# EMPATH

*The Complete Guide for Understanding and
Leveraging on Your Special Gift Whilst Protecting
Against Manipulation (Contains 3 Texts: Empath – A
Guide on How to Understand and Leverage Your
Special Gift, Empath – How to Protect Against
Manipulation & Chakras)*

W0006656

## Adam Johnson

# Empath

*A Guide on How to Understand and Leverage Your Special Gift*

# Table of Contents

# **Introduction**

Thank you for purchasing "*Empath*: A Guide on How to Understand and Leverage Your Special Gift". If you are reading this, you are likely curious about your Empath gift. In fact, you might not even recognize it as a gift just yet. Empaths who are not in control of their gift often discover that it is the source of much pain and stress. After all, feeling others' emotions and feelings so deeply can make them feel as though they are your own, and you can become an energy sponge to anything if you are not careful!

This book is designed to help you understand that being an Empath truly is a gift. You will learn what exactly is a part of your gift and why it is so special to have it. You will also learn exactly how you can embrace being an Empath and use it to your advantage, instead of feeling as though you are living at the mercy of this gift.

It is important that you first and foremost realize that something that affects you so powerfully only does so because it truly is a powerful gift. Being an Empath is something that can bring you a great deal of benefits and blessings in life that non-Empaths simply cannot understand or experience in their own lives. They may think that because they can feel empathy they understand, but the reality is that empathy is much different than actually being an Empath.

Please take your time as you read this book, and embrace each chapter before you move on to the next. It is not uncommon for your ego to become overwhelmed and tune out or flat out and refuse to receive the information being given to you in this book. You will need to take your time and fully understand each section before you can embrace the next one in the way that you need to. Each chapter has been written for your highest understanding and benefit, so please take your time and enjoy.

# Chapter 1: Gifted Empath

"I'm an Empath". Those three words can be hard to embrace when you are truly an Empath, and they can even become associated with negative situations. "I can't go out because I am an Empath; it is too stressful to be in crowded places." Or "I have to minimize my time speaking with others because I am an Empath, it can be hard". You may even find that you struggle to make friends on a deep level because you take on too much of their energy and it can be exhausting and sometimes even painful. This is a very common situation for an Empath who has not taken control of their gift. For this very reason, many people believe their gift as an Empath is not a gift at all. In fact, they may think it is a curse or something else terrible that is created to make them suffer. This is simply not true.

If you are an Empath, you experience many different things that non-Empaths would not comprehend. It is much different than empathy itself. You don't feel *for* others. You *feel others*. When you are around people, you can feel their energies and you may struggle with absorbing those energies like a sponge. It can be difficult and stressful, and if you are unsure as to what you are doing, it can be draining and frustrating.

Before you understand exactly how your Empath gift is truly a gift, you should understand exactly what it entails. You may be surprised to realize just how many of your "symptoms" in life are actually associated with being an Empath. The following are some of the common symptoms experienced by an Empath.

## People Call You Sensitive

As an Empath, you have likely been called sensitive numerous times throughout your life. People often say it like it is a negative thing: "oh quit being so sensitive!" or "you are too sensitive!' are things that you have probably heard on a regular basis. You have likely also heard other things around this general message. It is probably something you hear often, and may even be the root cause for you not feeling confident and empowered about your gift.

## You Feel Other's Emotions

This is the most common sign of being an Empath. You don't just feel for others, but you actually feel the emotions of other people. You may even feel them physically: their sadness may show up in you as tears, their anger may show up in you as a pounding heart or higher blood pressure, so on and so forth. This is one of the biggest symptoms of being an Empath and is generally the first thing that people notice when they realize they are an Empath.

## Negativity is Overwhelming

Most people dislike excessive negativity, but for you it is extremely bad. It may even physically hurt when you are in the presence of excessive negativity. It is hard for you to be in the presence of people who are negative, especially on a regular basis. It can make you physically ill and can be very hard for you to endure. You may find yourself avoiding these individuals.

## Crowded Spaces Are Overwhelming

When you are in crowded spaces, it almost feels too "loud" even if there is no sound at all. You try to avoid the feelings of others, but somehow you absorb them like a sponge. You cannot help the fact that you are constantly taking on the emotions of those around you. Even excessively joyful emotions can be exhausting because you are feeling enough for a room full of people!

## You Have a Strong Intuition

Because of your ability to read the emotions and energies of others, you likely have a very strong intuition. You can call out predictions, and you are often right. Your gut instinct is very powerful and you probably listen to it often, or at least you should. It is probably hardly ever wrong.

## You Struggle with Pain Intolerance

Just as you can emotionally feel more than others do, you likely physically feel more, too. You may struggle with a lower pain tolerance than others, and this may contribute to why you are called "too sensitive" on a regular basis. Unlike others, physical pain hurts you way more. Stuff that may not affect others at all will be torturous to you.

## You Avoid Negative Media

Just as you struggle to be around excessively negative people, you also struggle with negative media. You likely avoid all negative media, especially if there are graphic images or videos attached. When you see something, you can't un-see it and it may affect you on a deep emotional and physical level. You can literally become traumatized from the things you see and hear.

## You Can Call Out Liars

Likely thanks to your strong intuition; you are easily able to tell when someone is lying. You can call it well before anyone else can. If someone lies to you, you know they are lying. You may not feel confident enough to call them out for it, but you know they are. You may start to avoid these people like the plague because their lying energy is too much for you to handle.

*You Are Sensitive to Medications and Stimulants*

Again, just like your emotions are highly sensitive, so is your body. Because of this, you may feel the effects of medicine and stimulants like caffeine much more than the average person does. You may find that you can't even ingest high levels of caffeine or any at all because of what it does for you. You may also have the same situation with medications.

*You Develop the Symptoms of Others*

Something that you may notice is that you develop the physical feelings of others, too. Empaths are not just prone to emotional baggage, but to physical stuff too. You might find that if someone around you says "I have a headache" you immediately develop one, too. If they were to express a pain in their ankle, you would get one too. You can physically feel the symptoms that people describe to you, and they may even become problematic.

*You have Frequent Lower Back and Digestion Ailments*

Empaths often complain of having frequent lower back aches and digestive ailments. These are the physical symptoms that you experience as a result of taking on too much negative and uncomfortable energies. You can usually eliminate these by clearing your energies and reclaiming your peace.

## *People Come to You with Problems*

People seem to sense that you are capable of hearing their problems and helping them, and so they come to you like moths to a flame. They want to tell you everything, and may not understand what makes them feel so open around you. As a result, you may find that you are constantly attracting even more overwhelming and negative energies to yourself, and you can't find out why. All you know is, it is very difficult to deal with it all!

## *You Are Often Fatigued*

Taking on as much energy and feelings as you do can be exhausting to anyone. You are not immune to this. As a result of all of the energies you take on, you will often find you are chronically fatigued. You will likely find that it gets even worse after a day where you have been surrounded by a large number of people, even in a joyful celebration or similarly happy setting.

## *Your Inner Life is Vibrant*

Even though your external life may be stressful, your internal life is likely vibrant and enjoyable. You probably compensate for your stressful external life by creating a positive and powerful internal life that makes you feel comfortable and happy. As a result, you may find that you are quite introverted, even if you long to be an extrovert.

## *You Are Sensitive to Sensory Feelings*

As previously mentioned, you are not just prone to taking on emotions. You can take on physical sensations, too. Loud music, excessive touching, and other sensory feelings can be overwhelming for you. Sometimes you may crave them, other times they may simply be too much for you to handle.

## *You Can't Multitask Well*

If you try and multitask, you likely find that you simply tune out or can't handle it. Doing too many things at once requires too much of your energy. Because you are constantly absorbing the energies around you, it is hard to add anything else into the mix. When you do something, you have to focus on one thing at a time in order to be successful with it.

## *Your Environment Reflects Your Sensitivities*

You have likely been an Empath your entire life, and therefore you are well aware of all of your sensitivities. As a result, you have likely shaped your environment to meet your needs. The aesthetics and feel of your surroundings are likely ones that bring you comfort and meet your sensory and emotional needs to help prevent you from becoming over-stimulated.

## You can "Feel" the Days of the Week

One symptom that you may have but are unaware of is that you can "feel" the days of the week. Each day of the week may have a unique feel, and you tend to feel it. As a result, if one day "feels" like another, it may through you off and become exhausting for your energy.

## You Listen Well

Because of your Empath gift, you are probably a great listener. You may even feel guilty to say "no" if someone needs you to listen to them, and therefore you find yourself in many situations that may be difficult for you, but you are too polite to remove yourself from the situation. You can truly feel what the speaker is saying, and that makes them feel understood and cared for, which is something most people crave, including yourself.

## You're Easily Bored

You have a high level of creativity and passion and need to stay active constantly in order to prevent yourself from getting bored. Even though you may not like overly stimulating environments, you also don't like under stimulating ones, either. Ones that provide you with the opportunity to focus on one thing with minimal external energies and stay on track with something that is allowing you to use your creativity are optimal.

As you can see, there are many symptoms that go along with being an Empath. You may find that many of these are things you experienced but never realized, or simply didn't know were a part of being an Empath. These symptoms may seem troublesome or burdensome, but trust that being an Empath truly is a gift, and you're about to find out why.

## The Gift of Being an Empath

It can be hard for you to understand why being an Empath is a gift, but the reality is that there are many reasons why it is such a gift to be an Empath. In fact, there are so many that it is hard to narrow it down to one good reason. Just like there are many reasons why it can be hard, there are many reasons why it is a blessing, too.

First and foremost, being an Empath generally means that you are a natural healer. It may seem as though the "broken" people gravitate towards you, but that is because they can feel that you can help them. And, you can. Your hands, your voice, and even the things you do in life are all a source of healing. Many Empaths go on to do energy healing, massage therapy, or other healing professions in life, because they feel most comfortable and at service in these jobs.

Another wonderful gift Empaths experience is a heightened ability to experience life. You smell flowers more deeply than others, you hear music more beautifully than others, and you taste with more intensity. In fact, you can even work to increase your sense of smell and you will be able to actually tell when others are ill, which is an incredible skill to have. You can sense the potential dangers that are present long before others, too, which comes as a result of being more in tune with your sixth sense.

Even though you are prone to feeling deeper lows, and you likely know this from a very personal situation, you are also prone to feeling higher highs. You likely have a wonderful sense of enthusiasm about life and feel deep joy. You tend to be far more kind and understanding, as well as caring and compassionate towards others. This is true towards yourself, as well. You likely feel all of these nurturing emotions towards yourself, and therefore you enjoy alone time and the chance to unwind and de-stress as it allows you to recuperate from your day. In fact, you may even find that you *need* that time.

Another wonderful gift Empaths have is that they are generally highly creative. This is true not only in regards to art but also in the realm of experiences and situations. You may also notice creative possibilities ahead of you and how you can make the most out of your life.

As an Empath, you are powerfully capable of recognizing non-verbal cues. You can read the emotional cues of others, body language, and many other non-verbal methods of language. This is a great benefit because it helps you thoroughly read a situation and thus react in a way that is most appropriate. You can also use this gift to communicate with non-verbal beings, such as plants, animals, infants and even the human body itself. You may be able to mirror these cues to non-verbally speak with others, too.

Even though it may seem difficult, another wonderful benefit of being an Empath is that you can see right through people's lies or masks. You can tell when someone is being untrue or unfaithful, and you can clear yourself of the situation well before anyone else even realizes it is a problem. People truly cannot lie to you without you finding out about it virtually right away, because you are so easily capable of reading their emotions and non-verbal cues.

You may have felt up until now that being an Empath was a burden, and understandably so. When you are not trained to manage your gift, it can be hard to use it for the highest good. Still, it is a possibility. In this book, you are going to learn exactly how you can use your Empath gift for the highest good and gain the most out of it. By the end, you will know exactly how you can manage your gift and leverage it for good. In the meantime, you should take the end of this chapter as an opportunity to relax and truly embrace all that comes with being an Empath. Now is a good time to reflect on the symptoms you experience, acknowledge them, and start recognizing them for the gift that they truly are.

# Chapter 2: Embracing Your Gift

When you are an Empath, you can easily become physically and emotionally drained, which can quickly lead you to feel as though your gift is actually a burden. In fact, the first stage of being an Empath is feeling this burden. However, the next step is learning to care for yourself in a powerful way that will help you embrace being an Empath and feel better in the long run. This process is extremely important and you should take the time to learn how to truly master your self-care process. Doing so will greatly help you use your gift for the highest good of yourself and the world around you.

When you are an Empath, you have to really go the extra mile to take care of yourself. Because you feel stress and other overwhelming emotions so frequently and deeply, you must take greater measures to eliminate them from your energy body, and your physical body. There are many ways that you should take care of yourself to ensure that you are nurturing your emotional and physical needs. Doing this on a regular and routine basis will help you feel more relieved from your Empath symptoms and will allow you to start truly realizing what a gift this skill is.

One of the most important parts of caring for yourself is admitting who you are to yourself. Stepping out of the dark and openly and loudly admitting that you are an Empath, will release a great deal of stress you may feel around your Empath. You may feel fearful about sharing your gift with others which can create a larger amount of stress on its own. You can eliminate this by speaking your truth.

Next, you really need to make sure that you are resting deeply and thoroughly. Getting on a regular sleep schedule and incorporating rest into your daily schedule is important if you are going to feel relief from some of the struggles that can come with being an Empath. It can be beneficial to set a bedtime and a wake time and ensure that you do everything that you can to have a restful sleep between those hours. Additionally, make sure that you take regular breaks throughout the day to breathe deeply and relax to eliminate some of the stress that has built up from your day so far. Doing this will help you feel a great deal of relief, quickly.

Another thing you should do is avoid over-stimulating environments on a regular basis. It can be hard to avoid them altogether, but you want to try and avoid them as much as possible. When you are going to be in a stimulating environment, you should mentally and emotionally prepare yourself for the situation. Doing so will give you the opportunity to eliminate the amount of stress you may feel as a result of the stimuli around you.

One sneaky area of stimulation that people often don't realize matters is social media. In fact, the internet, in

ADAM JOHNSON

general, can be an over-stimulating environment. It is a good idea to unplug on a regular basis and give yourself a break from all of the energies that you carry from the internet. Just because you are not physically in the presence of these individuals doesn't mean you aren't absorbing the energies that are present!

In addition to resting and avoiding difficult environments, you should make sure that you have a regular stress-relieving routine in place. What you will do will vary based on who you are and what you like, so get creative with what helps you relax! You may wish to read a positive or empowering novel, take a warm bath, use aromatherapy oils, get a massage, or do anything else that helps you relax.

As an Empath, it is extremely important that you embrace having a powerful and positive self-care method in place. In addition to caring for yourself through regular measures, such as a healthy diet and regular exercise, you are going to want to have a strong de-stressing routine in place to help you release all of the energies you are absorbing and relax more.

In addition to taking care of yourself by de-stressing, there are many ways that you can actually prevent yourself from taking on too much. You can read more about them in the second book in this series, "*Empath*: How to Protect Against Manipulation and Empower Yourself with Your Unique Gift". Learning about how you can shield yourself against negative energies and protect yourself from absorbing too much is a powerful tool to have and it can greatly assist you in your journey as an Empath.

At this time, you should start thinking about how you can create a powerful relaxing routine for yourself. You should have an idea of how you can incorporate relaxation into your regular routine, as well as have days or times set aside where you will put more into completely relaxing. Ensuring that you are getting regular relaxation in will help you eliminate a large amount of the negative side effects of your gift and start embracing it as the gift that it truly is.

# Chapter 3: Understanding Energy

Once people learn how to embrace their gift as Empaths and understand how they can start relieving themselves of the excess energies, they often become curious about energy itself. You have noticed how powerfully that can affect you through your symptoms and experiences. So, if it can affect you that negatively, then naturally it must be able to have a powerful positive effect too, right? The answer is simple: yes.

When you are able to manage your Empath ability and relax from the stress that it can bring, you open yourself up to the ability to start understanding energy and using it for good. At this time, you may find that you are obsessive about learning more. In fact, that may even be what has drawn you in to this very book. Learning about how energy works is exciting, and it can lead you to amazing places in your life. As you learned, many Empaths go on to become energy healers, because of how powerfully it can influence their lives, and thus, they know how powerfully it must be able to work on others, too.

Getting into the energy research related with your Empath gift is important, but there is one thing that you should do before anything else. That is, you want to learn exactly how to ground yourself from energies. Doing this will help "root" you and keep you from becoming overwhelmed with the energies that you are experiencing. There are many ways that you can ground yourself, with visualization being the most popular method. You can use your creative mind to visualize yourself becoming grounded, or you can use the following as a guide or a starter:

*"Sit in a comfortable chair if you can, and place both of your feet firmly on the floor. Let your body relax into the chair and don't force yourself into any set position. Ideally, you should set your hands so that your palms are facing up. Imagine a bright white light piercing from the sun and down through your crown chakra, and out through the bottom of your spine then into the center of the Earth. Imagine that while your body is filling with white light, black negative energy is releasing through your palms and going away from you. Soon, your entire body will fill up with white light and you will be able to relax completely, knowing that the energies within' you are only positive and peaceful ones."*

If this visualization works for you, you may wish to keep it as your own. Or, you may wish to choose a different one that suits you better. Regardless of how you do it, you need to be sure that you have a strong grounding strategy to help you eliminate your energies and feel more connected to the Earth beneath you. Doing so will help you release all that does not serve you and feel more powerful in your existence.

Once you have learned to ground yourself, you will be able to move on to learning more about how other energies work. As an Empath, you are very clear on how powerful energy is. It is also a wonderful way to learn how to get control over your gift and stop having to worry about feeling like you are out of control. Energy work gives you the ability to protect yourself, heal yourself and others, and ultimately control the energy around you that is directly affecting you. The more you learn, the more exciting it can be.

Because of how in tune Empaths are with energy and feelings, it is not uncommon for an Empath such as yourself, to become almost obsessive about energy work. You may find a deep passion in it and even find that you are able to make a career out of it. There are many types of energy work that you can consider, and whether you do them as a career or just for personal use, it is actually a really good idea for you to learn and start using them either way.

As an Empath, you may find that you are drawn to perform work that is both healing and enjoyable. There are many ways that energy can be used to create a beautiful situation, whether you are looking to heal, manifest, or send certain energies in someone's direction. You can do a number of different things when you learn how to work with energy, which is one of the reasons why people are so deeply attracted to it. As an Empath, it is your Divine and inherent gift to be able to have an easier sense of navigating these powerful energy paths, and using them for the highest good of yourself and the collective good of everyone around you.

There are a number of different things you may wish to do with energy, so we will focus on exploring the primary ones in detail, now.

## Healing

As an Empath, you are fully aware that there is an energy body connected to people, and that this body has the ability to become inflicted with pain or illness. When you learn about energy healing, you learn how you can work with someone else's energy body, or your own, to eliminate these pains and illnesses and create a healthier energy body. As a result, people will end up leading a healthier life overall.

There are many reasons why someone would want to visit an energy healer. For example, they may be grieving, angry, traumatized, sad, ill, or otherwise feeling out of alignment. It is important to realize that if you go into energy healing, you cannot replace a doctor's place in a person's life. You cannot prescribe medicines or diagnose ailments or illnesses. However, you can go ahead and help that person work through energy blocks they may be having and even work alongside doctors as an additional means of therapy to help people through.

If you look into it, there are many different styles of energy healing out there. The most common one is reiki, but there is also chakra healing, shamanic healing, healing touch, qigong and more. As you search into energy healing, you will learn more about these different formats and how they may be able to enhance your life.

The best part about being an Empath and learning energy healing is that you don't necessarily have to heal others. You can learn these strategies simply to be able to heal yourself on a more regular and consistent basis. As well, these teachings often have information around how you can ground yourself and eliminate the impact of others' energy on yourself. When you are an Empath, knowing how to protect yourself from the energy of others is extremely important, as it helps keep you from absorbing everything around you and has the ability to make your environment a more comfortable place for yourself. Whether you decide to learn energy healing for your future profession, or if you simply want to learn it for yourself, it is a good idea to do so.

## Manifesting

This is where one of the most exciting parts of energy work comes into play. When you are an Empath, you have a strong ability to manifest virtually anything you want into life. Assuming, of course, that you are working for the highest good of the collective. If you aren't already aware, manifesting is the process of thinking something into your very own reality. It is some really fun stuff!

There are many strategies and techniques that are available when it comes to manifesting things into your life. As you start exploring through the various methods to do so, you will likely find one or two that feel most comfortable and natural to you, and therefore they work best. When they are working in full function, and you are working *with* those energies, you may find that the things you ask for in life come to you really fast! This is why this part of the Empath journey is so exciting!

When you are looking to start manifesting, you may want to discover some guided meditations that can help you visualize that which you desire to manifest. They will walk you through everything you need to do and know in order to bring your desires into reality. You will probably be very happy to find that it really is as simple as training your mind to think a certain way, even if only for shorter periods at a time!

Manifesting is a wonderful and exciting way to use your Empath abilities to bless your life. Even though you have an innate ability to heal others and provide wonderful services to others, it doesn't mean that you shouldn't be able to enjoy them from time to time, as well! Playing around with your ability to manifest is a great way for you to make the most of your life and have fun with your Empath gift, instead of feeling burdened by it!

## Mediumship

Empaths tend to be powerful mediums who have a strong ability to sense the spiritual realm. As an Empath yourself, you may or may not believe in this stuff. If you don't, then of course you won't be accessing this ability and you will likely not be too concerned about it. Don't worry, there is no need for you to dive into anything that makes you uncomfortable or that you don't believe in.

However, if you do believe in the spiritual realm, you may be excited to know that you have a very strong ability to connect with it. This is exciting because, you get a wonderful chance to tap into your Empathic feeling of "just knowing" and start using it. Before you do, though, you are really going to want to make sure that you are efficient and strong with your grounding skills. Interacting with spirit can be a difficult situation if you are not prepared to protect and block yourself from the energies that they may bring about. Remember that in *"Empath:* How to Protect Against Manipulation and Empower Yourself with Your Unique Gift" you will learn all about how you can protect yourself from unwanted energies and spirits that may come about.

Many people wish for the gift to be able to communicate with spirit, and as an Empath, you have a strong foot in the door when it comes to this. You may already have had experiences in the past with this, or you may just be curious and want to learn more. Whichever it is, you can learn more and trust that you will have a powerful ability to connect successfully with ease.

## Psychic Abilities

In addition to mediumship abilities, Empaths have a powerful ability to sense things before they happen. Because of your feeling of "just knowing", you may have premonitions or visions about things before they actually happen.

Without training, these visions or premonitions may just occur when they occur. However, if you take the time to learn how to tap into them, you may be able to teach yourself to have these visions "on demand" whenever you desire to. This is a powerful and wonderful opportunity for you to start predicting the future before it happens. Of course, chance and circumstances can result in the future being different from what is in your vision, but more often than not, you will likely find that you predicted correctly.

Just like with your ability to open up to mediumship skills easily, you can do the same with psychic abilities. So, if you have not experienced any visions or premonitions until now, it does not mean that you lack that ability. It simply means that you need to tap into it and learn how to connect to that part of yourself better and tune in more. As you do, you will likely find that predicting the future is easy and sometimes even fun!

## Sending Energy

Another wonderful thing that you may or may not know that you can do as an Empath is "send energy". When you send energy to people, you are giving them a specific vibe or sensation that you desire for them to have. Many people learn this as a means of remote healing and are able to energetically heal individuals from a distance. Others use this as a method of prayer and send good thoughts or energies in someone's direction to help them through a difficult time.

Anyone can send energy, but as an Empath, your energy is more likely to be felt and experienced by the recipient. It is easier for you to send your energy because of how powerfully connected you are to the energy source, and how easily it flows through you. As a result, you may often find yourself sending energy in other people's direction.

The most important thing to remember when you are doing energy work is that you don't want to ever neglect your self-care routines. When you start working with energy intentionally, it becomes especially important that you keep yourself on a routine of self-care. If you aren't careful, you can deplete your own energy levels which can result in exhaustion and even illness. This is why it is crucial for you to develop a strong relaxation and self-care routine before you get into energy work.

Once you are ready to get involved in energy work, you should start by creating a powerful grounding routine. As well, you should learn how to tap into source energy. This means that you visualize life force energy coming to you from the Earth, the sun, or however else you visualize source. Doing this will prevent you from sending your own personal energy and will keep you from feeling exhausted and depleted when you are done. It is important that you learn how to do this when you are getting started. After mastering grounding and tapping into source energy, you are ready to start using your energy for the highest good of the collective! You can do so in any way that feels best to you, whether that be healing, mediumship, manifesting, or otherwise. Remember, take your time and do what feels right!

# Chapter 4: Flexing Your Gift

Until now, everything is likely very new to you. You have always known you were an Empath, but it may be totally new to you that this trait is actually a gift or a blessing. As you read through this book, you are probably learning many things about yourself and your talent that weren't previously known to you. As a result, you are likely excited to flex your gift.

It is important that as you are learning about your abilities and skills that you take the time to learn more about each step. That is exactly the reason you are being prompted to take a break and practice at the end of every single chapter. You may think that this is only important when you are learning, but the truth is that you are actually going to need to practice this slowing down and embracing technique on a regular basis. The more you allow yourself to slow down and fully absorb what is meant to benefit you, the more you will actually be benefitted by it. This is a powerful skill you will learn as an Empath.

Over the next several days, weeks and even years, you are going to learn a great deal about your Empath abilities. The learning phase can last a long time, and you should be prepared for that. Eventually, you are going to move from beginner to advanced, and from advanced to mastery. As you excel through these levels, you will become more confident and empowered about your abilities and gift. In the beginning, though, it may all feel overwhelming. The best thing you can do is lay a solid foundation for yourself and practice these healthy "housekeeping" strategies on a regular basis. Doing this will prevent you from burning out or reverting back into a phase where you feel as though your gift is a burden.

Since you are likely quite new to all of this, we are going to go through some of the best things you can do to help you flex your gift and get used to it. Once you start getting used to it, you will start feeling guided in your own direction of how you should carry on. At that point, you should follow your intuition.

## Meditate

It is important that you meditate on a regular basis. This is a form of relaxation, but it is a form that you need to partake in often. Ideally, you should meditate every day. Doing this helps you in many ways. It allows you to disconnect from the world around you, but it also allows you to tap into your creative side. Most often when we meditate and clear our mind off clutter, we end up discovering some phenomenal things. You may even see energy around you or in your mind's eye. This is a great opportunity to reinforce that the energy is there and around you and that you have access to it at all times. When you meditate, don't try and use the energy or do anything with it. Simply observe it and recognize it for what it is.

## Relax Often

For the same reason you should meditate frequently, you want to relax often, too. Again, this is a good way to keep your energy from becoming depleted. However, it is also a great way to sit back and observe the energy around you. When we are excited about using the energies around us, it is not uncommon to want to manipulate them or play with them all the time. This can become exhausting though and can actually turn into stress for you. Instead, take your time. Sit back often and simply observe the energies. You can observe the energies of people, things, or simply the environment around you. Don't try and manipulate it or play with it, simply watch it and feel it for what it is.

## Start Small

Just like with your physical muscles, your mental and Empath muscles also need to be strengthened. For some people, they have unconsciously been strengthening them for a long time, so they may be able to come out of the gate with a strong ability to manifest or create anything that they want. For others, it may be a better idea to start small and work your way up. If you are reading this book, let's assume that the best opportunity for you is to start small.

You should focus first on easier things, like manifesting a free cup of coffee or for a specific feather to fall into your path. When you are learning to manifest, it is important that you learn to have faith that it will happen, which can be hard when larger items don't come to fruition quickly. The better you get at manifesting smaller things, the better you will be at manifesting the larger things in the long run. Of course, you can always go ahead and work on manifesting the larger things right away. It's just important that you realize that you are going to need to practice patience and faith until your skill becomes powerful. The more you manifest, the easier it will be. Eventually, you will find that you can effortlessly manifest what you are wanting in a very short time span.

## Ground Yourself Always

It is very important that you discover a grounding strategy that works for you and then you use it frequently. Doing this will help you alleviate the energies that you are holding onto and return yourself back to a state of peace. When you are learning to ground yourself, you may struggle at first. It can be hard to effectively ground and eliminate everything all at once. Because of this, you may find that you have to use your grounding strategy several times a day in the beginning. The better you become with it, however, the easier it will be for you to ground and effectively eliminate all pent up energies every single time.

There are many different types of grounding strategies that you can use, so you will want to search around for the one that works best. Previously in this book, you were guided through one, but there are several more you can consider. Some Empaths even like to wear grounding crystals, such as garnet or onyx, to help alleviate the energies and prevent themselves from negative energies becoming built up within' them.

You will find that once you start implementing and regularly using a grounding technique, you will have a much easier time managing the energies within' your body. You won't feel so bogged down or full of negativity that doesn't belong to you. Any emotions that are painful or uncomfortable will likely subside, which will make it easier for you to feel more confident in your ability to use your Empath gift for good.

## Take it Slow

You may feel compelled to learn everything all at once. Just like you want to start small with your manifesting, though, you want to go slow with your entire process of learning to cope with energies and learn to work with them. If you move too fast, you may fail to grasp some of the most important foundational processes required to help you master energy work without jeopardizing your own well-being as a result.

Going slow gives you the opportunity to master every single step along the way, which is important. Additionally, if you go too quickly you may become overwhelmed and suffer as a result. The best thing you can do is take your time, follow your intuition, and do what feels right. There isn't a recommended set speed for you to go, so long as you are going slowly enough that you are able to fully comprehend and master each step along your path. The better you master each current step, the better you'll do on all future ones.

## Give Yourself a Break

If you do run into a period where you feel overwhelmed, exhausted or drained, the best thing that you can do is take a break. Remember to practice your grounding techniques and then spend the rest of your time relaxing and meditating. Don't work towards any type of energy work or manipulation, as you will likely only make it worse for yourself. If you aren't careful, these energy blocks may manifest as physical ailments, which you definitely don't want.

For some, it is a good idea to schedule breaks on a regular basis. You may find that weekly breaks are the best opportunity for you to sit back and relax and keep yourself free from the overwhelm and stress that can come from working with energy too often or not taking regular breaks to revitalize yourself and your own energies.

Breaks don't mean that you completely disconnect from energy. As an Empath, you likely realize that you are always connected to the energy around you. However, it does mean that you would slow down from being involved in doing any work in the energy that surrounds you and take it easy. You would withdraw from intentional energy work during those days, and in doing so, you would give yourself the best chance to relax and rejuvenate.

## Journal Your Experiences

Whenever you are learning something new, especially something as powerful and profound as the energy work that you are involved in as an Empath, you should journal your experiences. There are many reasons why you would want to journal these, but ultimately it is an amazing way to track your path as you evolve along the way from beginner to master.

When you journal, you should write down things you have tried that worked for you, and note the things that didn't. You can note about certain experiences you had and how they made you feel, and virtually anything else that feels right to journal about. Doing this lets you see how far you have come, allows you to check back and remember what worked in previous situations, and sets you up for success in the future. It is a great way to recap the things that have happened to you and see how different life was then versus now.

## Practice Often

Just as with anything else in life, you are going to want to practice on a regular basis in order to gain the best skills in your Empath gift. The more you practice manifesting, energy work, meditating, grounding, healing, and anything else you desire to do with your gift, the better you will be able to use it. Just like a bicep muscle, the Empath muscle must be worked on a regular basis if you want it to be strong and useable. When you practice on a regular basis, you set yourself up for success and you fast track yourself from beginner to master.

There are many ways that you can flex your Empath gifts and start using them more effectively. The best thing that you can do is take your time and go steadily about it. As you practice more and more, you may discover certain things you prefer using or practicing over others. You may begin to notice other things about yourself, as well, that help you feel more confident in your Empath gift. If you haven't already, you should start practicing your desired Empath gift abilities and set yourself up with a regular schedule to practice everything that you have learned in this chapter. Once you are feeling more confident in these skills, you will be ready to learn to control them!

# Chapter 5: Controlling it

Although it may not seem obvious, there are actually large differences between flexing your Empath muscle and actually controlling it. When you are flexing it and learning to strengthen and grow it, you are generally not completely in control of it. You may be encouraging things to happen or working with energy, but you are likely not completely aware of how you are making it work or when it is going to work. That is why journaling is such a smart and powerful thing to do when you are flexing your Empath abilities. It allows you to become more aware of the trends in your skills and when it worked and when it didn't.

At this time, you are also going to be gaining control over your life in general. Until now, you may have felt as though you could not control what made you feel comfortable and what made you feel uncomfortable. You may not have been in control of the things that caused you to feel negative, so you controlled them by avoiding them. Ultimately, you were living your life by running away from the results that were arising from your Empath symptoms. Now that you are learning to control them and use them at your own will, though, you will find that it is a lot easier for you to control your entire life, too.

## Controlling Your Empath Gift

In the previous chapter, you learned several ways that you can practice using your Empath gift, which is an important foundation in learning to control it. The more you practice, the more you will be able to actually control your gift. Controlling your gift through energy work is a powerful way to regain control over your energy, mentality, and emotions in a way that allows you to prevent yourself from absorbing any energies you do not desire to carry with you. It also allows you to learn how to shape your life to your desired patterns and enjoy it in a way that benefits you. Ultimately, instead of being controlled by your Empath gift, you will control the gift and use it in whatever way you desire.

Some Empaths choose to use their gift for a greater purpose, such as energy healing, mediumship readings, or other similar energetically charged reasons. Others prefer to simply learn how to manage their gift and live a life as free of its influences as possible. Whichever way you decide to live your life and use your gift is unique to you, and you should feel confident and comfortable in whatever decision you choose.

## Controlling Your Own Life

As you become more in control of your Empath gift, you will learn that you also become more controlling over your personal life. You will no longer feel as though you are at the mercy of your Empath symptoms, and will have more control over what you can do. Things that once affected you and made you run away in fear of becoming drained or exhausted will now be things that you can confidently accomplish without worrying about the outcome.

Now that you are no longer worried about how you are going to manage life around your Empath symptoms, you will be able to make choices and plans that reflect your wants and desires, and not what your Empath symptoms state you can and can't do. You will not fear that doing certain things will lead to excessively negative outcomes for you. Instead, you will feel empowered to take control and lead your life your way.

Learning how to get control over your Empath gift is the best opportunity to gain control over your life. The two come together hand-in-hand as you learn more. The more you get into practicing controlling your Empath ability and grounding yourself from energies around you, as well as shielding yourself against them, the more successful you will be in your life in general. You will no longer live at the mercy of your gift, and instead, you will live in complete confident, control over it, knowing that you can use it to your benefit when you need to and that you can set it aside when you want to.

At this time, you should have already been practicing getting in control of your Empath gift. You may not be a master yet, but you may already be able to recognize areas of your life that have been relieved and enhanced based on your ability to control your Empath life. If you are journaling, you may even be able to reflect back on your entries and realize just how far you've come and how much more confident and in-control you are now versus when you first started! Knowing this is an incredibly liberating feeling and you can confidently feel assured that it will only continue to get better and better.

# Chapter 6: Increasing Clarity

This is the part of your Empath journey where you realize you are in control and you can start using your gift as a gift, even if you're only limiting it to your own personal life. At this time, you should be able to tune out of unwanted energies and emotions and control how you are affected by people and situations around you. You may not be one hundred percent in control, but you are at a place now where you can see the light and you know that you are going to be completely in control sooner, rather than later.

At this time, you will start gaining clarity around your gift and the world around you. Instead of constantly feeling drowned by thoughts and emotions of others, you will be more in tune with their emotions and thoughts in a positive way. You will be able to read a room effortlessly and not feel overwhelmed in any way, shape or form. Now, or soon, you will be able to be present with others' emotions without feeling burdened by them or absorbing them in any way that is negative to your own energy. Occasionally you may find that you need to check in with yourself and ground, especially after a particularly emotionally intense situation, but for the most part, you will be able to naturally deflect unwanted emotions and energies and stay more in tune with yourself and your own needs. If you do pick up something unwanted by accident, you will be able to easily and quickly eliminate it from your energy field and carry on your way.

Even if you have decided that you only want to use your Empath gift in your personal life, you will start finding your gift enhancs your own life in amazing ways that enable you to get the most out of life. There are several areas in which being an Empath can positively affect you, and you will start recognizing that now.

## In Business

As an Empath, you may find that your gift is powerful in the world of business. Because you are able to read people and understand their emotions, you know how to speak to them in a way that makes sense to them and allows them to understand you. With your ability, you have an advantage when it comes to making and closing deals, getting promotions and raises, and staying on people's good side just by being yourself. If you run your own business, you may find that when you gain control over your Empath gift that your business explodes and you start doing phenomenal with it. This is quite common for Empaths who gain control over their gift and learn to channel it in positive ways.

## With Friends and Family

Now that you no longer suffer from the emotional and physical baggage that comes from feeling the intense feelings that others feel, you may find that your personal relationships grow more. You will now be able to channel your Empath abilities to tune in when you need to and be helpful when you need to, but you will also feel confident enough to tune out and say "not this time" when you need to, as well. You will have a greater understanding about self-care and therefore, you will be able to consider yourself more in these relationships where Empaths tend to ignore their own needs and feelings. You will not carry the weight of others feelings and therefore you will be able to listen and help out in a more powerful way, since you will not become emotionally or physically ill as you listen to their stories and feel their emotions. This can increase the bond between you and others and make your relationships even more enjoyable for both of you, as well as more positive, too. You may feel even more fulfilled since you are now able to get the most out of your relationships without feeling withdrawn or guilty as though you cannot be the type of support you long to be for others. You will also not be so likely to have that feeling of resentment towards others who tend to come to you often with their problems, and you will understand it more and be able to channel your response in a more positive manner.

## Around Strangers

When you are an untrained Empath around strangers, it can be hard. You are hearing and feeling the unwanted emotions and feelings of others and you may not know how to stop. As a result, you may have found that previously it was hard to go anywhere

where there would be unknown people. You would never know what their emotions would be like or how you would feel when you left. Now that you are in control, though, you will find that it is a lot easier to be around strangers because you can now effectively tune out or deflect their unwanted energies and ground yourself more efficiently. As a result, you will find it a lot easier to do regular errands or other tasks where strangers will be involved.

## In Crowds

Previously, crowds may have been extremely tough. So many emotions in one area can be stressful! Now that you are better at controlling your Empath gift, though, you are likely going to have a much easier time when you are in crowds. This is true for whether the crowd is a group of people you know or people who are strangers to you. Being able to channel your Empath gifts in crowds means that you will no longer be prone to struggling in these crowds and that it will become easier for you to interact with those around you. You will not feel drained or exhausted at the end of your experience; instead, you may even feel revitalized and energized. This means that you can start engaging in experiences that involve crowds again, and not feel as though you have to hide or stay away from these situations.

## When Driving

Driving is a time when you can easily become affected

by others emotions. You can see other drivers easily, and you may experience road rage which can leave you feeling stressed and drained. When you learn to ground yourself, though, you no longer feel the effects of these people who are spreading their negative emotions around the road. Instead, you can ground yourself and feel confident in your driving abilities and know that you are safe in your own care.

## During Conflict

A major pain point for Empaths is conflict. Because you take on other's energy, it can be very stressful and emotional for you to enter a situation that involves conflict, especially if it is with someone that you deeply care about. When you start learning to take care of yourself and channel your Empath gifts, you begin to find ways to endure conflict in a manner that ends positively for all involved. Instead of walking away feeling as though you have been robbed of your energy and often getting the underhand because you are too drained to stand up for yourself, you will walk away feeling confident that the situation was handled as justly as possible. You will feel more empowered when speaking up for your rights and your beliefs, and you may begin to feel less concerned about how others feel about you, because you will feel more confident about how you feel about you. When all is said and done, you will be able to quickly ground yourself from the energies and you will be able to feel more relaxed and less drained in the end. Unlike in the past, you will recover quickly, instead of being affected for a long period of time afterward.

There are many situations in your life that will be positively enhanced by you having the control over your Empath abilities and clarity over how they entwine with your life. You will learn how you can stay clear on situations and prevent yourself from reacting in a way that disempowers you or takes away your confidence. Instead, you will be able to act with confidence and clarity and feel empowered that you are working for your best interest and the best interest of all that are involved.

If you haven't already, you should start looking at the ways that you can use your gift to positively enhance the way that you lead your life. Even though you have control over them, you may find that there are still other ways that you could use them to your highest good. Taking a little time to start paying attention to what your natural responses are to certain situations and learning a way to make them more positive can be empowering and powerful in regards to helping you lead a more peaceful and happy life. You may find that there are several outdated and unnecessary things that you have been doing that you would now like to stop. You can do so easily, by thinking about new ways that you would prefer to respond and then practicing responding in these new ways when those situations arise!

# Chapter 7: Normalizing It

The final part about embracing and leveraging your gift as an Empath is to learn to normalize it in your life. For this part of the process, you will be learning how to make it something more comfortable and effortless. Instead of having to think about your desired response or how you could use your gift, you will simply be able to use it and benefit from it. You will no longer have to put effort into the process of remembering to tap into your gift, it will become second nature.

This normalizing process is a major part of stepping into your full gift as an Empath. It allows you to eliminate ever having to worry about being an Empath again, because it is natural and easy for you to manage it on a regular basis. You will never have to worry about feeling at the mercy of your gift again because you will know what to do if it ever spirals out of control, which will be rare because you will so be in control.

When you reach this stage, it is not uncommon to feel like "oh yeah, I'm an empath!" because you have become so used to it. It will be natural for you to tune into energy when you want to or when it benefits you and tune out when you need to or when the energy would be negative to you. You get the best opportunity to enter a situation that will be as peaceful as possible for you on a nearly full-time basis.

You should realize that you will still feel emotions. Being a normalized or naturalized Empath does not mean you suddenly become void of emotions. Instead, it means that you will only feel the ones you intend to feel or the ones that are meant for you. You will not pick up on the energies of others, or feel immediate reactions to the energies you do pick up on. At one time, you may have lashed out or become drained and exhausted in the face of the energies of others. You may have avoided public situations or even crowds of familiar people. Family gatherings, house warming parties, and dinner parties may have all been situations you would have never dreamed of attending, because at one time, you knew you would leave the gathering feeling overwhelmed and exhausted for several days to follow. In that time, you may have struggled to understand where the exhaustion or unwarranted negativity was coming from. You may have felt emotions that seemed to have no known cause and felt confused and frustrated as a result. The constant influx of emotions that were coming into your body may have caused you to feel heavy and uncomfortable.

But now, none of that happens. Or at least, not very often. Now you are so accustomed to your life as an Empath, that you can go into a crowded room of familiar or unfamiliar people and feel empowered and energized. You do not pick up random energies that you do not want and you do not absorb emotions that do not belong to you. You can read the emotions of others, but you do not feel victimized by those emotions. They do not harm you in any negative way. You know how to effortlessly ground yourself and deflect the emotions and feelings that do not serve you. All of the physical symptoms you picked up from others or carried as a result of all of the stress have disappeared, and if they do happen to reappear, you know exactly how to eliminate them again. Because you have already mastered the process of being an Empath, it is easy for you to regain balance in your life quickly and restore your energy and confidence.

# Chapter 8: Maintaining Your Gift

Mastering your gift and maintaining it are two different things. When you master it, it is easy for you to live a life in harmony with your gift. You will reach a point in your life where it becomes normalized as we discussed in the previous chapter. However, there are things that you need to do, following the normalization of your Empath gift in order to make sure you stay in control and that you don't end up back in the same shrinking patterns that you were in when you viewed your gift as a burden or as a struggle to maintain.

There are some primary things you need to do to maintain your gift, many of which you will recognize from when you were learning to control your gift in the first place. Being able to manage the gift of being an Empath is what will allow you to continue living your life in perfect harmony. You will not have to worry about your gift taking control over your life once again, because you will know exactly what to do if you are feeling unaligned.

## Check in Regularly

An important part of maintaining your Empath gift is

checking in on a regular basis. You will want to do this at least once a day, but preferably twice. The best times to check in are in the morning and in the evening. Doing this will give you the best opportunity to reflect on what has affected you at the most transitional points in your day.

When you first wake up in the morning, you will be able to recognize residual experiences that may be resting inside of you, as well, as what we have been holding onto in our mind tends to come to life in our dreams. You will then be able to intentionally release these feelings and return yourself to peace and harmony for the rest of your day.

Bedtime is also a great opportunity for you to check in because you will now be conscious of the experiences that you have had throughout the day that may be taking up space in your energy body. You will be able to recognize what these experiences are and how they are affecting you and then consciously and intentionally let go of them so that you can have a restful sleep without being affected by the unwanted or negative energies that were taking up space in your mind and body.

## Meditate Daily

In addition to checking in on a regular basis, you should meditate at least once a day. Once again, the best times for meditating are first thing in the morning when you are still in a sleepy state, and right before bed. However, you should not make a habit of meditating yourself to sleep every night, because you may damage your meditation practice. Doing this can cause you to always become sleepy and fall asleep when you are meditating, which takes away from the value of a strong meditation practice.

Meditating on a regular basis allows you to just be with energy. You eliminate the stress of judgment and of having to feel in control and you give yourself permission to just be. Doing this gives you a wonderful chance to stop feeling as though you always have to be in control and simply experience life and energy for what it is at the moment.

## Breathe Deeply

Relaxing frequently is important, but while you are relaxing you should be very intentional about your breath. Breathing deeply gives you the opportunity to fully relax to a level that no other activity can provide. You allow yourself the ability to completely achieve a restful state in your body and feel rejuvenated through the breathing patterns. A good breathing pattern you can try is breathing in for 4 seconds, holding the breath for 6 seconds and breathing out for 8 seconds. Doing this will help you completely eliminate the excess air from your body and with that, you can visualize any stress and unwanted energy leaving with the air, as well.

Breathing deeply is a great way for you to center yourself and achieve inner harmony quickly. If you are in a situation where you are struggling to ground yourself, start by having centered and intentional breathing. This will help you quickly regain control over your emotions and your entire being and be able to start acting with intention once again, and come back into your power center overall. You should do this on a regular basis, preferably daily. If you are in a situation that brings you discomfort, you should go ahead and start the relaxation process with deep breathing.

## Ground Intentionally

A big part of normalizing your Empath abilities is no longer paying attention to your need to shield and ground yourself, because you don't necessarily need to. Only, if you do need to. It is very important that you continue to ground yourself on a regular basis with great intention. Doing this will allow you to regularly eliminate excess energies in your body and come back into your center intentionally.

You should never leave your energy maintenance on autopilot; because you will quickly fall out of alignment and become unbalanced. Intentionally grounding yourself on a daily basis, or as needed if you find you need to ground more, will allow you to make sure that you are eliminating all unwanted energies and feelings that you may have absorbed during your day. Even when you are a master at managing your Empath gift, you may still discover that you come into situations on a daily basis where you catch yourself absorbing energies from those around you.

## Release Emotions That Do Not Serve You

Even emotions that you have organically felt and have not absorbed from other's need to be managed. You will want to make sure that you are releasing emotions that do not serve you. Just as you do with the emotions of others, you can do this intentionally through grounding and meditation. This doesn't mean that you should simply jump ahead and eliminate all emotions that don't feel good to you. Instead, it would mean that you should work through and permanently eliminate those that do not serve you for your highest good.

Carrying on emotions, even your own, can be exhausting. As an Empath, you may find that the energy that goes into deflecting and eliminating unwanted energy and emotion can take up a lot of effort, even when you master it. Because of this, it is important to stay on top of your own emotions, too. Keeping everything in check will prevent you from reaching a burnout stage where you feel drained and exhausted from the energies you have encountered, including your own.

There are many ways that you should continue to manage your Empath gift even after you have mastered it. In fact, even during the process of mastering it, you will want to continue paying attention to these important maintenance factors. Doing so will enable you to have a more harmonized existence with your gift and will prevent you from reaching phases or stages where you feel like you are out of control or shrinking back into a situation where your gift is taking over you, instead of you being in charge. Learning to manage your entire energy house can be hard, but with regular maintenance, you will eventually find it to be easy. It is important that you learn these habits early on so that it is easy for you to carry on over time.

# Conclusion

Being an Empath is a gift, but it may not feel that way when you are not in charge of your special gift. You may find that without controlling it, you are often drained, exhausted and feeling unwell. These symptoms may even present themselves in your physical body. It can be hard for you to manage at first, but as you learn how to do so, you will eventually learn to understand the power of your gift and how you can use it to enhance and leverage your life. You may even choose to use your gift to help others in their own lives. Many Empaths go on to make a profession out of their talents. Others prefer to keep it to themselves, and that is okay too.

As an Empath, it is important that you learn to gain control over your abilities in order to prevent your gift from controlling you. When you are out of balance, you may feel as though you are reverting back to those original sensations of being unwell as a result of carrying too much energy of others. The more you practice controlling yourself and your gift, though, the easier it will be for you to regain balance in these situations.

It is important that you understand that empathy itself is different from being an Empath, and those who are not on the same path as you will not understand what it is like to be an Empath. They may judge you as being highly sensitive or emotional, and they wouldn't be wrong. Still, it can feel hurtful when people say this with a negative connotation. Learning to ground and protect yourself against these people's unwanted energies is a good way to eliminate the harmful vibrations they can cast your way.

I hope that this book was able to teach you how to understand your gift fully and embrace it in a way that allows you to leverage your life. I hope by now you realize that being an Empath truly is a gift and that it is a powerful gift that you should use in your life. At the very least, you should use it to your own highest benefit. If you want to, though, you can certainly use your gift to benefit others, too!

The next step is for you to discover exactly where you are in your unique path and what you should do next to control it. You may not be at the very beginning stages of this book, but rather, you may find that you fall somewhere in the middle of where you are at in controlling your gift. That is completely okay. Understanding the entire process is important for helping you build a solid foundation and stay in balance along the way.

If you enjoyed this book, I ask that you please take the time to rate it on Amazon. Your honest feedback would be greatly appreciated.

Thank you, and best of luck in your journey!

# Empath

*How to Protect Against Manipulation and
Empower Yourself with Your Unique Gift*

**By: Adam Johnson**

# Table of Contents

# Introduction

Thank you for purchasing *"Empath:* How to Protect Against Manipulation and Empower Yourself with Your Unique Gift". This empowering guidebook was written to help teach you how to protect yourself against situations that drain your energy and leave you feeling exhausted and vulnerable.

As an Empath, you might have likely run into many situations where you have been the victim of manipulation and other negative effects of energy vampires and energy abusers. People can sense that you are sensitive and that you are a giver, and you may struggle occasionally to assert yourself and protect yourself against these people. In fact, you may even struggle a lot. Being an Empath can be hard, especially when you are unsure about how to protect yourself against these energy attacks.

This book has been carefully written to ensure that you get the best information possible to help you protect yourself against this manipulation and these people. As you read this book, you will learn about important methods and techniques that are important to your ability to protect yourself. You will also learn about things to look out for, including how to identify a manipulator and an energy vampire who does not have your best interest at heart. As a result, you will have an even better ability to protect yourself and prevent the effects of these manipulators.

As you read, you will learn how you can take control over yourself and assert yourself in a peaceful and respectful but powerful way that virtually forces people to respect your boundaries and space. You will be able to protect yourself from that vulnerable feeling that you are prone to when you are feeling stuck between a rock and a hard place. In the end, you will have a much easier time being peaceful and in harmony in your life.

Being in tune with your Empath abilities and thoroughly understanding how to protect yourself and your gift is vital to living a healthy life. Each chapter has been designed to help ensure that you get maximum benefit and that you are able to quickly and easily apply your new skills. Please enjoy.

# Chapter 1: Grounding Yourself

You will hear this time and again, but grounding yourself is crucial and highly important when you are an Empath. Grounding yourself is a powerful opportunity to alleviate yourself the energies you are infected by and regain control over your life. When you ground yourself, you let the negative energies dissolve from your energy body and you let yourself become cleared and balanced once again. This eliminates you from being affected emotionally and physically from symptoms of stress and increases your ability to feel in harmony and oneness with yourself, your emotional and mental state, and your soul.

There are many ways that you can ground yourself, some of which take longer and are better for clearing larger or harder blocks, and others that can be done quickly. Ideally, you should have multiple grounding strategies in your Empath "tool kit" to help ensure that you are always prepared with something in every circumstance. Sometimes you may find that you need something large and powerful when you are really struggling, so, you will want to have a really strong tool in your kit. Other times, you may just want to do routine housekeeping; so, you want a simple but impactful grounding strategy. Other times still, you may find that you need a quick and rapid method to ground yourself immediately, in a state of emergency or dire need. Having something to satisfy each of these needs is a perfect way to ensure that you can ground yourself at any time that you need to, and in a way that will powerfully move the unwanted and negative energies out of you.

What you choose to do for grounding exactly will vary. You may be someone who likes to engage all of your senses, or you may be someone who works best with visualization. You may struggle to visualize with your eyes closed, but have an easy time visualizing the things around you as grounding tools. It is normal and completely fine to have different needs when it comes to grounding yourself. The most important thing is that you recognize and then address these needs so that you are able to ground yourself in the most efficient way possible for your unique needs.

In addition to ways to ground intentionally when you have an energy block or build up, there are other things you can do to maintain your grounding and stay in a powerful state of oneness. The following ideas are things you can do to ground yourself on a consistent and regular basis, as well as ways that you can ground yourself in a pinch if you find your energy out of balance.

## Drink Water

The body is made up of about 75% water, and yet people don't tend to drink enough to stay hydrated.

When your physical body is out of balance, it can be easy for your emotional body to quickly follow suit. In order to prevent yourself from becoming unbalanced, you can ground yourself through drinking water. If you need to ground yourself intentionally, you should drink slowly and mindfully. Taste every sip, and recognize how the water feels as you are drinking it. Take time to notice what the glass feels like in your hand, and how it feels against your mouth. Be slow and intentional about each sip, and allow it to ground you.

Not only is water one of the most important elements in our body, but it is also one of the five major elements of the Earth (Water, Earth, air, fire, and spirit are the five). Water itself teaches us that we must stay down to Earth and fluid. We must stay grounded but go with the flow. When we consider this aspect of water as we are drinking it, it can further increase the benefit of grounding through water.

## Manage Your Diet

Again, if your body is unbalanced your mind will be, too. You need to make sure that you are staying on top of your physical well-being so that you are always in balance physically. This will greatly contribute to your emotional and mental well-being, too.

Managing your diet very much aligns with what may be considered obvious. Make sure that you are getting all of your vitamins and nutrients, keep your mineral intake up, and eat as many fresh foods as you can. The better your diet is, the more balanced your hormones will be, and the more balanced your body, mind, and spirit will also be. It is important that you take the time out everyday to nourish your body with whole and healthy foods. Always try and stick to organic, non-GMO whenever possible.

## Balance Energy

This may seem obvious, but it is highly important. You need to balance your energy on a regular basis. You can do this in many ways, but most people use visualization as their strategy. You can visualize the negative energy or energy blocks within you leaving your body either through your feet or your hands, and allow them to completely exit. In their space, you should imagine a bright white healing light filling in. When you are done, you should feel much lighter and calmer as a result. It is important to balance your energy and remove your negative energies regularly and intentionally.

In addition to balancing your energy by eliminating the negative and increasing the positive, you will also want to balance the masculine and feminine. An individual who is more of one than the other may find himself out of balance in a way that impacts him heavily in life. You may find this to be weird; you may feel compelled to be more of your own gender than the other. One may call to you more than the other gender does. Still, it is important that you balance out the masculine and feminine energies within you. This does not necessarily mean that if you are masculine by nature that you should act more feminine, or if you are feminine by nature that you should act more masculine. Rather, it means that you should open up to the Divine energies of both; and be aware of, and acknowledge them within your life. Accept and appreciate them, and make sure you pay attention to both. Both have something powerful and beneficial to offer you throughout your existence here on Earth.

## Sage Smudging

Once thought to be reserved for cultural traditions, smudging yourself and your surroundings is a great way to clear out unwanted energies and restore the positive energies in your environment. Sage has a powerful healing and clearing energy that allows you to not only cleanse, but also protect yourself and your space as well. It is the most commonly used herb in regards to smudging. You may use virtually any herb you desire, though.

If you are using herbs for the spiritual purpose of energy clearing, you may want to consider researching the ones you choose to use. You can use numerous herbs, and each has its own unique properties. You may even change what you use from one time to the next, based on what you need and what each plant has to offer. If you cannot access smudging sticks, you can easily use incense sticks as well.

## Regular Exercise

You are already aware that your bodily health directly affects your emotional and mental health, but are you aware of how much physical exercise can impact your emotional and mental wellbeing? When you exercise, you physically move built up energies and emotions out of your body. Think about it e-motion. It is energy in motion. Therefore, if you get into more motion, you encourage it to clear out and move on.

Getting into a regular exercise routine, gives you a chance to always keep your energies flowing and getting anything that is unwanted out of you - for good. It is beneficial not only to your physical health, but also to your overall wellbeing.

## Meditate Frequently

Empaths are constantly told to meditate, and it is for a good reason. As an Empath, you are frequently impacted by energies and you may find yourself wanting to manipulate them often too, as a means to protect yourself. Meditating gives you a chance to sit back and simply observe energy for what it is. You give yourself the opportunity to see the energy for what it is and eliminate all judgment of it being "good" or "bad".

Meditating also gives you the opportunity to clear your mind entirely, which can be healing on its own. Of course, you can never achieve a completely cleared mind, but you can clear your mind off judgment or anything that could be straining you from fully letting go of things. When you sit back and observe, you learn a great deal. You should meditate on a daily basis, ideally once in the morning and once at night.

## Exercise Creativity

Creativity is a powerful outlet for energy, especially ones that feel blocked or unbalanced. There are many ways to be creative, and as an Empath, you are likely to be talented in a surplus of these areas. You should set aside time to exercise your creativity on a regular basis. Be intentional about setting aside this time, and ensure that you are getting the most out of it. Let your mind wander and do what feels right. Don't try and force your creativity or go in with a plan, just let things be and see what happens as a result. These are often the most creative and breath-taking pieces of work that people create. It is also one of the most therapeutic ways of releasing energy that has built up inside of you and getting yourself back into a healthy flow.

## Balance Your Chakras

You have seven main chakras in your body, and each of them needs to be maintained so that they don't become unbalanced. These energy centers are full of spiritual power, and they run from the bottom of your spine all the way up to the crown of your head. Each one has a unique purpose and meaning, and each one has the ability to become over used or under used. It is possible for just one to become unbalanced, but if one does, often all become unbalanced as a result.

Balancing your chakras is important, as it allows you to feel more balanced and in harmony in general. There are many ways that you can balance chakras, but the most commonly used and easiest way is to visualize each one in its respective color and imagine the color becoming strong and clear. You can find many chakra charts online that will help you gain a better understanding as to where each chakra is, and what color it is associated with. They are easy to remember once you learn them, as they match the colors of the rainbow!

**Try Yoga**

Yoga is a wonderful and powerful way to meditate through exercise. It gives you an opportunity to physically move out energy, without exerting yourself too much to do so. Most yoga poses are intentionally used to get energy moving, and help your physical and energy bodies operate more functionally and in harmony. Yoga poses are designed to help open up your chakras and keep you flexible and fluid.

You do not have to be a yogi master in order to practice yoga on a regular basis, but you certainly should practice it frequently. Even if you just stick with a beginner's video or course, it is a good idea to make it a regular routine in your life, so that you are frequently benefiting from all that it has to offer. Yoga is a powerful way to keep energy moving and work in harmony with it with your physical and energetic bodies.

## Go in Nature

Nature has a powerful way to make everything feel better. When you are out in nature, it is almost impossible to prevent yourself from grounding within your surroundings. The peaceful way that nature powerfully impacts us is in a way that cannot be replicated virtually anywhere else. Being around trees and plants that are deeply rooted, water that flows smoothly, and wildlife in itself is a healing situation. It eliminates you from highly energetic and busy areas and gives you a chance to take a deep breath and let your soul do the same.

Every single Empath should make a point to spend some time in nature on a regular basis. Doing so will increase your ability to feel relaxed and at peace with your environment. When you step into nature, you can almost feel yourself grounding immediately and without intending to do so. Therefore, when you intend to do so, it has a profound impact that can alleviate just about any energy block you may be dealing with.

## Laugh Yourself Healthy

There is a significant benefit behind laughing on a regular basis. It can be easy to go several hours or even days without laughing, especially as an adult. We have a tendency to become so serious about our lives that we forget to take a break and laugh and enjoy ourselves. If you are having a hard time lifting up your spirits and alleviating negative energies from your body, laugh. You can watch funny videos, read a funny book, watch a comedy, or listen to jokes. It doesn't really matter how you trigger your laughter, as long as you get yourself laughing long and hard. You may even consider fake laughing until you start laughing for real, and then just going with it.

## Crystal Energy

Many people who have the Empath gift are intuitively attracted to crystals. You may even find that you are attracted specifically to the ones that have the ability to heal you in ways that you need to be healed, or, you may be attracted to ones that resonate on any number of other levels that are profound for you. Crystals carry wonderful vibrations that can help you achieve almost anything you desire. Whether you want to increase your digestion, love easier, protect yourself, or do any other number of things, you can almost always find a crystal that will help you.

There are many ways to use crystals for their healing energies. You can meditate with them, you can hold them in your hand and rub them, you can pray over them, or you can even simply wear them throughout the day. How you use a crystal will be unique to you and your desires. However, it is common that once you use them, you will not go back. They have a powerful ability to heal us on a spiritual level. One that is highly important to Empaths.

## Essential Oils

When you are struggling with certain ailments, essential oils can have a powerful impact to help you. The best essential oils for grounding include: ylang-ylang, clary sage, lavender, and jasmine. There are many others you may wish to use, as the list is almost limitless.

It is important that you pay attention to what essential oils you are using and where you are getting them from. Not all oils are created equally, so you will want to make sure that you are getting high-quality ones that are going to be safe to use. You should never ingest oils, and you should research each new oil before using it. For some, you can safely use small amounts on your skin. For others, you need to use a carrier oil to prevent irritations or burns. Also, there are certain people who should not use certain essential oils. You can prevent an accidental disaster by thoroughly researching a new oil before you start using it.

## Earthing

Earthing is a wonderful and easy method to quickly ground. People should do it on a regular basis, even daily if possible. Earthing is simple, and it has been proven to benefits people who do it. All you have to do is take off your shoes and socks and touch the bare Earth with your feet. Ideally, you will have to stand on dirt and grass, not cement. Doing so will open you up to the Earth and allow you to powerfully and easily ground into the Earth. This is a wonderful way to bring balance to your energies and harmony to your life.

## Professional Energy Healers

If you are ever deeply struggling with energies, and feeling as though you really can't get them flowing, or there is a certain energy you can't dissolve on your own, there are professional energy healers out there that can help you. Professional energy healers are trained to use the energy field around you and source energy to get everything flowing. There are many methods of energy healing, from reiki to qigong and aura soma. You can follow any path you desire when you find a professional energy healer; based on what you think will work best for you. The most important thing is that you find someone who feels comfortable for you and who can do what you need done in order to get your energies flowing again.

Grounding yourself is a powerful and important tool when you are an Empath. You must put energy and intention into grounding every single day. You may find that sometimes you need to ground more than others. This is normal, as life is constantly changing and you, too, are constantly changing. It can be beneficial to you to have several tricks up your sleeve, including ones that you use on a regular basis, and others that you use when you are struggling more than usual. Knowing exactly how you can clear out energies that are unwanted is important; as it will help you maintain your physical and energetic bodies and stay in harmony as much as possible. If you are still struggling with a particularly difficult situation, you may wish to seek professional assistance with that particular situation. Doing so can greatly help you eliminate the unwanted energies and return to harmony. Even energy healers need energy healers, so you do not need to feel uncomfortable about asking for the extra help.

# Chapter 2: Energy Shields

Energy shields are a great way to prevent yourself from taking on the energy of others around you. There are many different styles of energy shields, and like grounding, it can be a very personal and unique experience. Some methods may resonate more with you than others do, and that is completely okay. You should listen to your body and do what feels right for you, as this will give you the best chance to use a strategy that will be most efficient for your needs.

When it comes to energy shields, you can use physical tools to help, or you can rely on your visualization abilities. There are many different types of shields that can be used, and often you can use a variety of shields at once to create your desired effect. There is no right or wrong way to shield yourself against energies, as long as you are doing something to help protect yourself against everything that is unwanted.

## Visualization Shields

There are many different styles of shields that you can visualize to help you, what you choose exactly will depend on your needs and your preferences. The following shields are common ones used by Empaths, and you can likely find a lot of benefit from them.

### The Mirror

To employ the mirror shield, you want to imagine yourself being encapsulated in a silvery-white bubble of energy. Then, you should imagine that the energy is like one-way mirror glass. You can see out, but from the outside, it is reflected back upon itself. This is a great way to reflect other's own negative energies back to themselves while simultaneously preventing you from absorbing them.

### Blended Spikes

If you are in a situation where you want to blend in with the world around you and don't want to stand out in any way, you are going to want to use the blended spike shield. This shield is similar to the mirror shield in the beginning. You start by creating a bubble of silvery-white light around you. Then, you imagine that large spikes are drawing out from your bubble into the world around you. After that, you should imagine that the rest of the bubble creates spikes in towards you. This creates an evenly blended energy field that allows you to go relatively unnoticed in your environment.

## *Protection Shield*

If you need a quick and powerful protection shield, you can simply imagine the silvery-white bubble around you. Then, you should imagine it getting thicker and more powerful. You can then fill the inside of the bubble with intentional protective energies and ensure that you are safe within it. Doing so will stop other energies from coming in towards you and keep you safe from the outside energetic world.

## *Intentional Energy Shield*

Perhaps you don't want to shield yourself against negativity, but rather you want to shield yourself against something else unwanted. Or, you only want to let a specific energy type into your own personal energy field. To do this, all you need to do is imagine a bubble of energy around you and set your intention. You may wish to color the bubble with what feels right for you. For example, if you only want to feel and experience love, you may wish to color the bubble green like the heart chakra, or pink like rose quartz. Also, if you want to experience only creative energies, you may wish to color it orange like the sacral chakra. Setting intentional energy shields allows you to prevent unwanted energies from coming in by only allowing in certain energies that you have intended for, to come in.

To eliminate a shield once you are done with it,

simply imagine it dissolving away. Otherwise, it will protect you for some time. At first, you may feel as though your shields are not as protective as they could be. This is common in the beginning when you are first learning how to create shields and make them work. Eventually, though, you will get the hang of it and you will know how to make powerful shields that protect you in virtually any situation. The most important thing is that you practice on a regular basis and become used to what your own shield feels like and how it works for you. Again, this is a very unique experience, so it is important that you make it personal to you so that it works best.

## Crystals

Since crystals have their own energies, you may have already guessed that some of them have wonderful protective traits. You can get crystals for virtually any use, including protecting yourself. There are certain crystals you may wish to keep around you in order to help shield your energy, but the following are some of the most common ones:

- Black Obsidian

- Black Onyx

- Celestite

- Citrine

- Kunzite

- Quartz

- Peacock Ore

- Black Tourmaline

- Smoky Quartz

There are many more that you could use, but these are the easiest to find and are most common for protecting yourself against negative and unwanted energy. You can use these stones in a number of ways, just like with grounding. You can wear them, keep them in your pocket, keep them next to your bedside or on your desk, or just keep them nearby in general. There are many ways that crystals can be used to protect you and otherwise bless your life. How you choose to use them will depend on what is comfortable to you and what feels most effective.

## Angelic Shields

If you have ever heard anything about the spiritual realm, you will know that there are ascended masters, archangels, and guardian angels. These individuals actually have a powerful ability to shield you against unwanted energies. You can simply call upon them and they will come help you. If you are struggling to feel them, you can visualize their wings wrapping around you and taking care of you as you deal with a particular situation or feeling.

The most commonly called upon archangel for protection is Archangel Michael. He is considered the protection angel, and he can shield you against anything that is unwanted or harmful. He can be recognized by his royal blue and royal purple lights that you may see around you in the room or in your mind's eye when you are working with him. If you are unsure of what to say, you can simply say "Archangel Michael, I am calling on you to please protect me with your protective shield now." That is all you have to do. After you ask, Archangel Michael will arrive and he will protect you emotionally, energetically, mentally and maybe even physically from the situation that you are in.

The archangels, ascended masters, and guardian angels are powerful for helping us in many different circumstances. As an Empath, you may wish to learn more about them so that you can gain access to their powerful abilities. Having these higher beings around is a wonderful way to enhance your life and ensure that your efforts and wishes are met as confidently and powerfully as possible.

## Trees

If you are struggling with your own protection methods, you may wish to go out and practice in nature. Being around trees, in particular, seems to have a powerful ability to help people increase their energy work and master it in a much shorter time. Trees are such wonderful energy and wisdom stores, and they have so much to offer. If you are seeking to ground yourself and protect yourself from hardships and unwanted energies, doing your work in the trees can help increase your success in your practice. Of course, it isn't always possible for you to be around trees, but when you can, it is a good idea to take advantage of this time.

When you are in a wooded area, you can imagine what it feels like to be surrounded by trees. Imagine that they are all standing together to shield you from all that is harmful to you, and that they are protecting you and nurturing you against those energies. You may wish to communicate with the trees, either through talking or thoughts. Doing so can help you tap into powerful wisdom that can assist you in your journey as you learn to shield yourself from unwanted energies.

There are many ways that you can powerfully shield yourself against the unwanted. Whether you want to visualize the shield, use physical tools to shield yourself, or call upon help from the angels or trees, there is always a way to get a powerful and effective shield put around you. Shielding yourself allows you to deflect unwanted energies and prevent yourself from absorbing them into your own energy body. As an Empath, it is important that you learn how to prevent yourself from absorbing everyone's energies if you want to live in balance and harmony.

Remember, shielding yourself is a personal experience and you may want to take your time to find the things that feel right for you. You should follow your intuition as it will guide you to the things you need most. As you practice, you will find that certain techniques work best for you, and you get the best results from them. This is best, as it means you will end up with a very powerful and custom shield that can protect you from virtually anything.

# Chapter 3: Energy Cleansing

Energy cleansing is somewhat like an intense form of grounding, but is something that should not be written off simply because you already have a grounding technique. Grounding mainly focuses on eliminating unwanted energies, while energy cleansing focuses more in bringing in the wanted energies. You accomplish this to a degree when you put up a shield, or you set boundaries on what energies you want to let into your life, but it is important that you spend some time each day, or at the very least each week, cleansing your energy.

Just as there are many ways to ground and shield, there are many ways to cleanse your energy, too. You should do one method at a time, but you may wish to use various ones throughout your life, as each has an ability to heal and clear different areas of your life. These energy clearing methods are ones that you can and should do on a fairly regular basis to keep your energy clean and clear.

## Cut Cords

As an Empath, you may have heard the phrase "etheric cords" before. Etheric cords are energy cords that connect you to other people, things, or situations. When you find that you are taking on a lot of energy despite something being a part of the past or someone no longer being around you, you may be suffering as a result of these cords. Even though you are not in the presence of the situation or person, you are still experiencing the energy body from them.

Cutting your cords is fairly simple. You start by getting into a meditative state and imagining yourself somewhere that is peaceful and comfortable for you. Then, you imagine the person or thing that you would have cords connected to. It may be an old work place, an ex-spouse or friend, or any other number of things that did not serve you well on an energetic level. Once you can clearly see yourself and them, you can start to imagine the etheric cord that runs between the two of you. How you cut the cord will be unique to you. You may wish to imagine a giant pair of scissors cutting it. You may wish to use a saw and hack them off, or you may wish to do something else. The most important part is that you see the cord being cut completely. Once it is cut, you should imagine your own cord connecting back up to source, so that it can cleanse and replenish that unique energy line.

After you cut the cords, you should feel a great sense of relief as you are no longer affected by that person's energy body. Instead, you are in complete control once again, and you will not continue to suffer. You may still think about that situation, which is common. However, you will not likely feel excessively emotionally charged or uncomfortable anymore, as the unwanted energies will no longer be present.

## Clear Your Aura

Everyone and everything has an aura, which is essentially your energy body. The aura extends far past your bodily limits, and follows you everywhere you go. When you are an Empath and you have a tendency to take on other people's energies, you may find that you are struggling to clear your aura. It can become full of unwanted thoughts and energies.

Clearing your aura is simple, and effective. It can quickly eliminate the residual energies that are in your energy field and help you restore your natural balance. You can clear your aura in many ways. You may wish to imagine a white ball of light in the center of your body that gradually grows and pushes all unwanted energies out of your aura until your entire aura is filled with the white healing light. Or, you may wish to imagine a large washcloth literally cleaning off your auric field. Doing this is a great way to eliminate those unwanted energies that linger for long periods of time and affect you even long after you realize what is happening.

## Mind Your Thoughts

Your thoughts are a powerful energy source, and they have the ability to add to the unwanted energies you have when you are an Empath. These can weigh down your energy field, your auras, your chakras, and your physical body. When you are unaware of your thoughts, you are likely having many that take you back into past painful situations. The best thing you can do is learn to become mindful and pay attention to your thoughts. Immediately dispose of any that do not serve you.

At first, you may find that being mindful is difficult and that you struggle to gain control over, or even focus on your own thoughts. This is natural and normal. As you practice and take your time to build your awareness and mindfulness practice, you will find it easier to check your thoughts and do your best to keep them as positive and helpful as possible. Doing this will help keep your internal energies clear and will also help you quickly clear out external energies that may affect you.

## Balance Chakras

When you work with your chakras, you can heal and balance almost anything. We won't go too deep into detail, as you have already learned about the chakras and working with them in previous chapters, but you should note that they are a powerful way to cleanse energies, as well as to ground and protect yourself.

## Sacred Spaces

A great way to cleanse energy is to have a sacred space. This may be your bedroom, or a room that you go to where you keep the energies extremely clear and positive. You can decorate it however you want with things that make you feel good, and you can use it as a location that you go to when you need to clear your own energy body. This would be a special place that you can relax in or meditate in, and it will help you stay in peace.

When you have a sacred space, you should make sure that you do not let any negative energies come into your space. If for whatever reason they do, you should clear it through smudging or other space clearing strategies as soon as possible. You should also take care to do regular cleansings of this area, as just like your own energy body, the energy field in your sacred space can slowly develop stagnant or unwanted energies, as well. The more empowering and peaceful you keep this space, the better it will be for you when you are looking for a place that will keep you relaxed and comfortable.

## Sea Salt

It has long been known that sea salts, particularly Pink Himalayan Salts or Celtic Sea Salts, are phenomenal for their cleansing and healing energies. Did you ever hear about how chefs throw a dash of salt over their left shoulder to do away with the devil?

That is for the same reason as you should use salts in your life: it is a powerful clearing tool when it comes to remedying unwanted stagnant or negative energies.

You can use salt in many ways, as it is a very versatile piece. Perhaps you are already aware of Himalayan Salt lamps, which are a wonderful opportunity to get a calm and comforting glow while also gaining the added benefit of having a powerful healing salt in your immediate surroundings. You can also put salts in your bath, which is another great way to cleanse yourself. If you prefer showers, there are Himalayan salt bars that you can use on a semi-regular basis to help cleanse yourself. As well, you can eat or ingest salts in any way to gain the benefits of them. Salts are extremely adaptable, and can be used in several ways to achieve your desired outcome. You should use them as a means to clear your energy when needed.

There are many ways to cleanse and clear out your energy field. After you do, you would want to imagine it being purified with white light or any other colored light that feels empowering and comforting to you. Your energy body should always feel balanced and peaceful. It is easy for your energy field to become unbalanced, especially as an Empath. The above methods are wonderful ways for you to clear out these unwanted energies and return to harmony.

It is important to realize that unwanted or stagnant energies are not always the result of an outside source. Sometimes you may arrive in this situation from your own internal situations. Perhaps you are out of balance for too long, or you are not feeding yourself with positive thoughts and inner words. You should always pay attention to any outside factors, as well as inside factors that are contributing to your emotional situation. Knowing exactly what is causing it will help you clear it out easier and more efficiently. Then, you will be able to return back to your peacefully balanced state.

# Chapter 4: Meditating

You already realize how powerful and important meditating is. It is a great opportunity for you to eliminate yourself from the situation of judging or forcing energies, and gives you the chance to just be with your energies and the energies around you. The effects that regular meditation can have on you are powerful and profound. Having a regular meditation practice can truly help you change your life, especially in how you regard energy and how it affects you. As well, it gives you a chance to sit back and recognize things that you may not otherwise realize if you are immediately within that energy or emotion.

As an Empath, it is even more important for you to meditate frequently. This practice has a strong purpose in everyone's life, but even more so in your own. There are many ways that meditating will help you, including eliminating stress, enhancing your inner peace, and bringing you closer to enlightenment.

## The Exact Benefits of Meditating

When you meditate on a regular basis, you have a better chance of eliminating your excess stress levels. Meditating has been proven to reduce stress levels exponentially, more so, if you practice it on a regular basis and teach yourself to do it effectively and well. At first, meditating may be hard, but once you get used to it, you will notice an incredible difference in your meditation practice. As a result of the reduced stress levels, you may also notice an increased performance in your business and in your physical activity. Your relationships will also become more profound and impactful, and you will feel a better ability to provide and receive value from your relationships.

Meditating is also known for helping individuals build up their prefrontal cortex in their brain. This part of your brain is responsible for impulses, self-awareness, and self-discipline. When you build up and strengthen this part of your brain, you become more creative, productive, and you also enhance the efficiency of your cognitive processes, too.

In addition to helping with stress and building up important parts of your brain, meditating can also help you achieve enlightenment. This is a stage of your life where you are in harmony with yourself, and your ego no longer controls you as deeply as it once did. While we can never completely void ourselves of ego, we can become aware of it and thus develop a control over it that will help us lead a more mindful, peaceful and harmonized life. This results in you having a happier life where you can truly feel confident in being yourself and feel comfortable in your own skin.

Finally, when you take on a regular meditation practice, you bring yourself a greater ability to be truly happy in your life. The combination of decreased stress, increased self-love and mental awareness all works together to help you feel more empowered and happy in your life. You will feel more at ease, lighter, and you will likely feel less impacted by or stressed out by certain situations in your life. You will have an easier ability to "bounce back" and continue in everyday activities, even during times of conflict or struggle. It will be easier for you to regain your happiness and peace within yourself.

## How to Meditate

Learning to meditate may seem difficult. Many believe meditating requires you to completely clear your mind, but this is not true. In fact, it's even impossible. You cannot possibly keep your mind from thinking *at all*. Instead, meditation is about freeing your mind of *ego*, eliminating judgment and sitting with yourself, your feelings, and the energies in and around you. You recognize what comes to you, and just as quickly it passes you by. When you realize you are too far off in thought, particularly thoughts based on judgment or ego, you simply return back to your centered space and carry on. You do not judge or punish yourself for getting side tracked, you simply let it be.

To start meditating, all you need is a comfortable and

relatively quiet space. Of course, you should never meditate when you are driving or doing something that requires your immediate attention. You can go ahead and find somewhere quiet and peaceful that does not require you to be paying attention to anything, and then you can start practicing deep breaths. You should use your breath as your center, and focus on it as much as you possibly can. The more you do, the more relaxed you will become. Then, you can close your eyes and soak in that relaxation. Again, thoughts will come, but they will go just as quickly. When you realize you are straying away from your center, simply focus back on your breath. You should be breathing in deeply into your diaphragm, and then emptying it again. You can practice yogic or pranic breathing at this time to help you stay intentional about your breaths.

You can meditate for as long or as short as you want. The "optimal" time is about 10-15 minutes at a time. You do not actually have to meditate for prolonged periods of time to gain benefits from it. In fact, it is better to meditate for short periods, multiple times a day, instead of for one long period once a day. This helps bring you back to your center regularly, which has a powerful benefit. At first, you may find that you are only able to comfortably meditate for short periods of time, but over time it will become easier to get longer.

If you find out that you are particularly fidgety during meditation, or that it is too hard to stay still, you may want to try shaking it all out before you sit down to meditate. You can even do your meditation after physical exercise. This will help you keep yourself calm and relaxed without feeling as though you are becoming bored or agitated from being too still for too long. Eventually, it will be easy to stay still and meditate for longer periods of time. Even still, you don't need to work towards having a meditation practice that lasts several hours per day. Instead, work towards having one that lasts about 10-15 minutes at a time, and consider doing this about 2-3 times per day. That is the best way to gain the maximum benefits from this practice in your everyday life!

**Enhance Your Meditation Practice**

If you are struggling to find a way to relax well and really hone your practice, there are several things that you can do to make it easier. While you don't need any fancy equipment or accessories to meditate properly, sometimes it can be helpful to add certain tools to your practice to make it easier for you to meditate. The following are things that you may consider using to help enhance your meditation practice:

*Incense or Essential Oils*

For some people, having a specific scent in the room can really enhance their ability to meditate properly. You may consider using incense or essential oils, or even candles, to help create this calming aroma. The best relaxing scents are ones like lavender, rose, chamomile, and bergamot. There are many others that you may consider using as well, it will mostly depend on what you desire most. Doing this can help create a more pleasant scent in your immediate surroundings and increase your ability to feel more relaxed. This is especially true if you tend to be someone who is particularly drawn to nicer scents or whose moods are easily influenced by aromas.

*Meditation Pillow*

There are many types of meditation pillows you can purchase which can help you increase the comfort of your meditation practice. Meditation pillows are typically small pillows that are created to be placed on the ground so that you can sit atop of them and meditate. It makes your place of meditation more comfortable. You may wish to use a meditation pillow to help you get the best possible position to have a wonderful meditation practice that helps you enjoy it more. Sometimes meditation pillows are better than comfortable chairs or lying down; because they allow you to have more freedom in your positioning and placement, which can have a major impact on your meditation practice. As well, they are portable, so you can even meditate in places like the park, or elsewhere.

## Shawl or Blanket

For some people, it can be easy to become chilled when you are meditating. Sitting still for a long period of time can make you chilly, so then it can be hard for you to meditate well, since you are no longer comfortable. It is completely fine to cover yourself up with a meditation shawl or a warm blanket to keep yourself warm and comfortable when you are meditating. In fact, if temperature is any type of issue for you, it is recommended!

## Music

For some, having music makes it a lot easier for them to stay focused and meditate better. You may consider using a calming music such as flute music or piano music, or you may wish to use something like binaural beats. There are many different types of music or sounds you can meditate to, the one you pick will be based on what your preference is. The best is to make sure that there are no words, though, and that the tune is something calming and free of any noise that will cause you to feel anxious or otherwise energized.

## Candles or Low Lighting

Bright or harsh lighting can have a negative impact on your meditation practice. When you are meditating, you may want to use candles or lamps to lower the lighting and keep your surroundings a little less bright. Alternatively, you may wish to reserve your meditation for dawn and dusk as the ambient lighting is naturally lower due to the time of day. Having the lighting lowered makes it a lot easier for you to have a better meditation practice, without feeling overly stimulated by the lighting around you.

However, you may also want to consider meditating in the bright sunlight, with proper skin protection of course. There is something highly peaceful about the warmth of the sun on your skin as you are meditating. The vitamin D also offers you wonderful benefits as well, which increases the overall benefit of meditating in the sun. If you are a fan of the sun, meditating in it is a great way to increase your mood and empower your meditation practice.

*Guided Visualization*

If you struggle to meditate in the beginning, or if you are feeling particularly off balance, you may wish to meditate with a guided visualization or meditation audio track. You can find these in numerous areas, and they are a wonderful tool in helping you guide your mind. Because someone is verbally guiding you through the experience, you get the opportunity to stay focused on something and get a better idea of what it feels like to meditate and how you can use your mind space or imagination to invoke certain thoughts or feelings. Guided visualizations are a wonderful tool to help you increase your ability to meditate, especially if you feel that you are struggling. Even many people who have been meditating for several years still use guided visualization or meditation audio tracks to help them, especially if there is something particular that they want to meditate on or about!

Meditating is incredibly important, especially as an Empath. It allows you to relax and channel your energies into a more calming activity that has a powerful impact on keeping you calm in your life. It will help you alleviate stress, develop the part of your brain that is responsible for self-awareness, have an increased performance in relationships, work and physical activities, and become enlightened in your life. It will also help you foster more happiness within your life that is powerful, especially because Empath's tend to struggle to maintain happiness in life due to the constant absorption of others' energies. You should consider introducing a regular meditation practice into your life so that you can gain all of these benefits and protect yourself from the harms of stress and other unwanted energies that come from not taking the time to tune out from the world and tune in to listen to your inner body.

# Chapter 5: Energy Redirection

Energy redirection is a powerful tool that you can use that prevents you from absorbing energies and sends them in different ways, instead. When you redirect energy, you let the negative energy flow out and let the positive energy flow in. It is important that you constantly keep your energy in flow, as doing this gives you an outlet to eliminate what you do not want to store inside of you, and it gives you the opportunity to refill that now-open space with positive and desirable energies.

Energy redirection is a tool that you should use when you are in the presence of someone who is releasing their negative energy upon you. It is a powerful tool that allows you to recognize the energy but immediately release it without being affected by it in any way. It is similar to shielding, but rather than blocking the energy from ever reaching you, it allows you to read it and understand it, then send it away. This is a great opportunity for you to read a situation without absorbing it, which can be powerful when you are in need of some understanding without the emotional and physical baggage that can come along with that.

To redirect energy is simple, and you can do it in any place. When you are an Empath, you are already skilled at reading energy and bringing it in. The next step is to learn how to read it without absorbing it, and then turn it back out. As with anything related to your gift, this can be hard at first. However, you will quickly learn how to master this technique and you will be all the better off for it, as a result!

It is very simple and you will find that out quickly. To redirect energy, bring it in, read it, and then release it. You will need to have awareness about this and intentionally release this energy as well. The difference between grounding, shielding or energy cleansing and energy redirecting is that you are not absorbing anything in the first place. With grounding or energy cleansing, you are required to do so because you have absorbed the energy and you are now needing to rid yourself of it. With shielding, you are not allowing the energy to enter you, and therefore you may close yourself off from the ability to properly and effectively read the situation you are in. With energy redirecting, though, you can take in the energy, gather the "information" that you want from it, and then immediately release it. You will never be directly affected by it, but you will be able to gain important bits from it. That is the primary difference.

Learning to redirect energy is a powerful and important tool when it comes to having your Empath gift, and controlling it in an effective way. You can use it to help you better navigate public situations and any situations containing conflict, which is important to be able to do. It is a simple and short technique, but being able to take in, read and then release unwanted energies all in a quick and to-the-point strategy is a powerful way to really give yourself a chance to keep yourself from becoming drained or overwhelmed in public situations.

# Chapter 6: Recognizing Energy Vampires

Energy vampires are one of the hardest types of people for Empaths to deal with. If you have never heard of the phrase, you are probably wondering what exactly an energy vampire is. It is important for you to learn how to identify an energy vampire, understand who they are and why they are energy vampires, and learn what you can do against them to protect yourself from getting taken advantage of or being manipulated in unwanted ways.

## Who Is an Energy Vampire?

An Energy Vampire is a person who drains you. They may fill you with negative energies, or spend a large amount of time tearing you down. They like to blame you, tear you down, and take their jealousy out on you. Energy vampires are people who are insecure but work to make you feel insecure with them. They are bullies and like to create chaos in other people's lives for fun, because it makes them feel better about themselves and their own lives. Energy vampires are those who whine excessively, have short tempers, or tend to gossip excessively about other people. They are drama queens, and are virtually anyone who does not understand how to prevent themselves from constantly spewing toxic energy into the world around them.

These individuals are terrible for making you feel like you are unwanted or unimportant. They make you feel as though your gift is a curse, and these people may likely be the reason you have felt this way in the past. Energy Vampires are people who do not care about how they treat you or how you are being affected by them and their energy. They are not mindful of their energies, and many are not even aware that they have toxic behavior. Because of this, you may feel even more compelled to feed into their vampire vortex. They feed on your positive energy and seek to bring you down, often without even knowing it.

As an Empath, it can be really easy to get stuck in these traps. These people sense your "weakness" and use it as an opportunity to bring you down with them. They know that you will also come, because they know you are a sensitive person who cares deeply about others. Energy Vampires lack the ability to sustain their own life force, so they feed on other's life force energies. You will find that you have a strong guilt around these people because you want to help them but you feel guilty knowing that you are not helping yourself whenever you help them. Due to your nature, you will want to fix them or save them. The truth is, you cannot. The only person who can is themselves, and until they are willing to recognize what they are doing, they will have no desire to change.

Energy vampires can be absolutely anyone. They can be in your family, in your circle of friends, in your workplace, or even strangers that you come across in life. Energy vampires are not generally just one person; they are actually everywhere. As an Empath, you may find that you attract these vampires. Like a moth to a flame, they can sense your light and they want to feed off of it to fulfill their own inner lacking. It is not that these individuals do not have a light, it is that they cannot see their own light and therefore feed on the lights of others to be able to see a form of light within themselves.

As sad as the reality of an energy vampire is, you cannot let yourself become victimized by them. You need to learn to recognize them and then protect yourself against their negative energies. The very fact that they are unaware of their own tendency to be an energy vampire is what makes them so dangerous: they cannot comprehend what they are doing, and therefore they cannot stop.

## How to Recognize an Energy Vampire

At first, it may be really hard to recognize an energy vampire. They are master manipulators and can easily go under the radar when it comes to their manipulative and energy-sucking ways. The first question you should ask is "who do I know in my life that drains my energy?" Often, your intuition will shout out a few names at you right away. The best thing you can do is rely on your intuition and pay attention. Most often, your intuition will tell you that there are red flags long before you can rationally or logically sense them. Your inner voice is powerful at recognizing these people, and you should listen. The quicker you end or avoid an energy vampire relationship, the easier it is to get out.

If you are already in a relationship with an energy vampire and you are able to start recognizing it, you need to either get out or learn to protect yourself against them. These people are powerful at draining your energy and know exactly what to do in order to push your buttons and get inside of your head. This is what makes them so good at feeding their own light. They literally survive this way, and just as any survival instinct is strong, their ability to feed off of others is strong, too.

There will be many instances where you simply cannot completely exit a relationship with an energy vampire. If they are a family member or a boss, for example, you may be stuck in a relationship with them, at least for some amount of time. As a result, you are going to need to learn exactly what you can do to shield and protect yourself against their negativity and their energy-sucking ways.

## Protecting Yourself Against Energy Vampires

Many of the tactics you have already learned are powerful when it comes to protecting yourself against energy vampires. Shielding, frequently cleansing your energies and balancing them, energy redirection, and grounding yourself often is a great way to keep yourself from becoming completely drained. These strategies are powerful and are important, just as they are at any other point in your Empath life. However, when you are around energy vampires, you are going to want to use them more frequently. Additionally, there are many other things you can do to help protect yourself against energy vampires. With these types of people, you should combine as many of these strategies as you possibly can, as the more you protect yourself the less they will affect you.

*Take Frequent Breaks*

When you are in the presence of an energy vampire, you are going to want to take frequent breaks to protect yourself. Doing this gives you the perfect opportunity to take advantage of the alone time and do anything you need to in order to clean and clear your energies. You can spend this time meditating, grounding, strengthening your shield, or releasing the unwanted energies you have gained from the energy vampire. In addition to regular breaks during your visit, you should take regular breaks between visits. Try not to spend several days in a row with this person, unless it is absolutely mandatory. When you spend time together, it should be on your terms and when you have the energy to protect yourself against them.

## *End the Relationship, If Possible*

If you are struggling with the relationship and it is possible, you should consider just completely ending the relationship altogether. Doing this gives you the self-affirmation that you do not deserve their treatment, and it permanently ends their ability to have any power over you or to suck away any of your precious energies. In some cases, it will not be possible, but when it is, you should end the relationship. This will open up the space in your life for you to welcome in other people who are more thoughtful about their own energies and how they present them in the world.

## *Prepare Yourself to Be Around Them*

Before you spend time with a known energy vampire, you should prepare yourself to be around them. You should take this time to prepare your shield, and get yourself mentally and emotionally ready for their manipulative and energy-sucking tendencies. At this time, you can recognize what their common patterns are, and give yourself an idea of how you would like to respond in those situations. Having a plan already chosen gives you the best opportunity to respond in a way that is empowering to you and stops them from taking your energy away.

## *Let It Go*

It can be hard, but you need to teach yourself to let it

go. At first, you might struggle, but the more you practice letting go of their energies and the feelings you get from them, the better you will feel as a result. Remember, what they say, think or feel about you or anything else is not important to you. It should not directly affect you, and it really has nothing to do with you. Their thoughts and actions are a reflection of their own inner world, and if it is that negative, then it is really their own struggle, not yours. Nothing you can do or say will take that struggle away, they have to want it to go away and therefore be willing to put the work in.

## Don't Try to Save Them

No matter what way you slice it, you cannot save an energy vampire. They are people who generally don't want to admit what they are like, mainly because they likely just don't see it. You will not be able to make them see it, and you will not be able to change them. Trying will only make you feel exhausted and drained even more so than they already make you feel. The best thing you can do is let go of any ideas that you can save or fix them, and simply accept them for who they are. The faster you do this, the easier it will be for you.

## Don't Argue with Them

You should avoid arguing with energy vampires at all costs. They are often narcissistic and therefore believe that they do no wrong. They have a powerful way of manipulating the situation to make you feel as though it is your fault, or to twist your words and make you feel angry because they are not getting your point. The best thing you can do is avoid arguments or conflict with them. If they start the argument, do your best to dissolve the situation. Remember, agreeing that they are entitled to their opinion does not mean that you agree with their opinion. Again, accept them for who they are, and move on to focus your precious energy on more positive areas in your life.

## Have Clear Boundaries

When you are in the presence of an energy vampire, you need to have clear boundaries. You can create your boundaries before you start spending time with them to ensure that you are clear on what your boundaries are and how you want to assert them. In the next chapter, you will learn more about how you can assert your boundaries and your needs in your life as an Empath. It is crucial that you have clear boundaries and that you assert them around energy vampires, as this will help eliminate the effect they can have on you in the time you spend together, no matter how short or how long. Never back down on your boundaries, because an energy vampire will be able to discover what causes you to back down and they will manipulate you to back down at their mercy to get whatever they want from you. You have to be firm and stand strong in your boundaries and never settle for less.

## Get Perspective

Recognizing an energy vampire for who they are and gaining perspective is a great way to enforce your ability to let go of their negative energies and anything they may say towards you. Energy vampires are rarely targeting you directly. Instead, they are likely jealous or envious of you and your light and they wish to have what you have. Rather than taking the time to create it for themselves, they would rather simply feed off of your own light and success. An energy vampire is never specifically attacking *you* personally. They are opportunists who see a chance to fulfill a need of theirs, and they take it. Plain and simple.

## Affirm Your Own Sense of Self-Worth

In the presence of an energy vampire, particularly one that is rather bully-like, you may struggle to feel confident and positive around them. You may start to question your own sense of self-worth or leave the gathering feeling as though you are worthless or unlovable. None of that is true, and even though you may know it deep down, it can be a struggle to feel that way when they are in your presence or were recently in your presence. A great way to prevent this from happening is to affirm to yourself about your own self-worth. You should do this regularly when you are spending time together with an energy vampire.

Energy vampires are difficult people who feed on

other's energy to feel better about themselves. They are generally bullies, and they rarely know it. As an Empath, you may feel sorry for them or feel as though you can come to their salvation. The truth is, you can't. You must learn to put up boundaries and protect yourself against their manipulative ways. That starts by learning who an energy vampire is exactly, and how they affect you. Then, you can learn to recognize them and their energy-sucking attempts, and finally, you can protect yourself against them. The sooner you learn to protect yourself against these people, the better you will feel. Energy vampires are everywhere and they can be anyone. It is important to learn to prevent yourself from being affected by these individuals as soon as possible.

# Chapter 7: Assertiveness

Empaths often have a hard time asserting themselves. It can feel uncomfortable to say no or stand by your boundaries, especially if you feel like someone else is desperate or in need of help. We are often people who struggle to realize that we cannot help everyone, and that we need to be okay with that. It can hurt us deeply to feel someone else suffering and not be able to do anything about it. Having the ability to be assertive gives you the best chance to protect yourself from unwanted situations and preserve your own energy and wellbeing.

You have likely been in a situation in the past, where you put down your boundaries to serve someone else because you felt they needed you more than you needed the boundary. You may even have a problem with doing this often. Many times, Empaths find themselves in situations where they are doing an alarming number of things that they don't like, simply because they feel obligated to, in order to make others happy. Empaths are people pleasers due to their ability to read other's energies, and it can have a seriously negative effect on the Empath themselves.

Learning to assert yourself is an important tool that you need to get on top of immediately. The faster you learn to assert yourself, the easier it will be to honor your own boundaries and do only what feels good to you. You should not lead a life based on what other people need from you. Doing this will only make you drained and empty out your own energy reserves. Eventually, you will reach burn out and you will not be able to help anyone, yourself or otherwise.

There are many things you can do to practice being assertive. It is important to find ways that work for you and use them frequently. Learning this is important for your own health, and it is not something you can or should put off. You need to get on top of this, immediately!

## Become Clear in Your Boundaries

Many people struggle to assert their boundaries because they are unclear on what their boundaries actually are. If this is true for you, you need to start working on discovering what your boundaries are, exactly. You should sit down and think about things that make you unhappy or feel as though you are being taken advantage of. Then, you should create your boundaries around these. Once you are clear in your boundaries, you will know exactly what it is that you are asserting to other people.

## Learn to Say No

Saying no is hard, especially for Empaths. You need to learn exactly how to say no and how to be strong in your no. When you say no, it needs to mean something to people. If they persist and try to push against your no, or make you change your mind, you need to keep strong and stand in it. If necessary, excuse yourself from the situation to eliminate yourself from being affected by someone who is unable to accept your no. Remember, it is not personal when they can't take a no. They are likely desperate for your help, but you need to feel confident that you are not the person to help them if it is a situation that makes you uncomfortable. Someone out there will be comfortable with helping them and they will be able to find that person. Have faith in that, and stay firm in your boundaries.

## Clearly Outline Your Boundaries if They're Crossed

If someone starts crossing boundaries, you should be clear that they have done so. Telling people what your boundaries are, gives them a chance to understand them and respect them. If they don't know, they can't respect them. Some people push by nature, but if you were to point out that they are pushing, they would stop. You need to make sure that you are always asserting your boundaries and that people know what they are. If they don't stop pushing your boundaries, you should be clear about what will happen as a result. For example, maybe you won't help them anymore or you no longer want to be their friend.

## Avoid Those Who Continually Cross Boundaries

Some people will constantly cross boundaries. The

energy vampires, to be exact, will constantly cross boundaries. The best thing you can do is avoid these people and then take all of the measures as outlined in the previous chapter to protect yourself from these people. The more you avoid these people, the less likely you will be put in a situation where you know they will push boundaries. If you are in a situation with them, you should prepare yourself and get an idea of what you will do when they start inevitably pushing against your boundaries.

Being assertive can be hard, particularly for those who are gifted Empaths. Since you can feel the energy of others, you can often feel the desperation or need for help. As a result, you may put down your own boundaries for the benefit of others. Only, this doesn't benefit you in any way. In fact, it doesn't even benefit the other person. People need to have boundaries, and other people need to learn to respect them. If you don't assert your boundaries, you will end up having resentment and you may lose good friendships simply because you couldn't speak up. In many cases when you assert your boundaries, people respect them. If they don't, they don't deserve to be a part of your life! Simple as that. If they are a part of your life and they continue to cross boundaries, you need to limit your time with them and practice asserting yourself tirelessly so that they eventually learn to back down. If you give in once, they will expect you to give in forever - and they will push until you inevitably give in.

# Conclusion

Being an Empath is a gift, but people may try to take advantage of you and your gift. The best thing you can do, is learn how to protect yourself against being taken advantage of or being manipulated by others. It can be hard, especially if you are feeling overwhelmed or drained in the beginning. You may even need to take a break and give yourself a chance to restore your energies before heading back into situations where you know your energy will be drained.

There are many ways for you to protect yourself against these situations, including shielding, energy cleansing, grounding and more. This book has provided you with some powerful and necessary tools to protect yourself against draining situations and you should make sure that you practice all of them. How you choose to practice them will likely be personal to you, but ensuring that you have strong practices in place will have you on the path to success when it comes to restoring and preserving your own energies and feeling secure in your environment, no matter where you are.

I hope this book was able to give you a strong insight on what you need to do to protect yourself as an Empath, as well as get a solid idea of who you need to protect yourself against. Being an Empath can be hard, but once you learn how to manage it and take care of yourself, you will find that it is a lot easier. In fact, you may even come to fall in love with your gift and all that it has to offer your life.

The next step is for you to start practicing all of the techniques in this book and learning to powerfully protect yourself against unwanted energies and manipulation. Then, you will be able to confidently enter situations knowing that you will be in control and no one will be able to affect you in any unwanted ways.

If you enjoyed this book, I ask that you please take the time to rate it on Amazon. Your honest feedback would be greatly appreciated.

Thank you, and best of luck in your protection practices!

# Chakras

*Chakras for Beginners – The Step-by-Step Guide to Awaken Your Chakras and Heal Yourself*

**Adam Johnson**

the information in question by the reader will render any resulting actions solely under their purview. There are no scenarios in which the publisher or the original author of this work can be in any fashion deemed liable for any hardship or damages that may befall them after undertaking information described herein.

Additionally, the information in the following pages is intended only for informational purposes and should, however, be thought of as universal. As befitting its nature, it is presented without assurance regarding its prolonged validity or interim quality. Trademarks that are mentioned are done without written consent and can in no way be considered an endorsement from the trademark holder.

# **Table of Contents**

# About the Author

Adam Johnson has been interested in self-help and finding a way to be the very best person possible. In a world that is full of chaos and confusion, it is nice to take time away to take care of ourselves, and ensure that we are able to enjoy our lives. Adam realized that his life was full of things, things to do, things to see, things to meet with, but there was still something missing. That is when he began to do some research and came across the idea of chakras, the energy forces that are inside of us all and that. Now he devotes his time to meeting with others and helping them to live the fulfilled life that they deserve through various means, including taking some time to discuss chakras and how each one will influence your mood, your physical being, and even your health.

# Introduction

Congratulations on downloading your personal copy of *Chakras: Chakras for Beginner—The Step-by-Step Guide to Awaken Your Chakras and Heal Yourself.* Thank you for doing so.

The following chapters will discuss some of the many of the great things that you need to know about chakras. When the chakras are closed up or blocked, there are many different parts of your health that can begin to fail and while we may not realize it, we need to pin these up and get the balance back into our lives before we can feel better again. But when the chakras are opened and working freely, it is so much easier to enjoy life and feel fulfilled.

This guidebook is going to spend some time talking about the chakras. We will start out with some of the basics about what these are, before moving on to how each of the different chakras work, how to tell when the chakras are not doing their jobs well and are blocked, and then some of the techniques that you can use to help get your chakras back on track including color therapy, yoga, and so much more.

When it comes to getting your chakras in line, there is so much that you can consider. While most people will just ignore the signs and perhaps take medication in the hopes of getting those chakras in line, the best medicine is to work on the chakras in a natural way and realize that they are actually the part that is causing the problem. This guidebook will help you to learn a little bit more about your chakras and can get them back in line for you.

There are plenty of books on this subject on the market, thanks again for choosing this one! Every effort was made to ensure it is full of as much useful information as possible. Please enjoy!

# Chapter 1: What are Chakras and How Do They Pertain to You?

Do you feel that you are having trouble communicating with others? Do you feel that your thoughts are always in a jumble? Do you have issues with feeling bouts of anger and humiliation on a daily basis? If you are feeling any of these issues in your life, you may be dealing with an issue of a chakra or more out of line.

The chakras are our centers of energy, located right along the midline of the body. There are seven major ones, although some schools of thoughts about the chakras will include a few more of them as well. These chakras are going to all work together and when they are in great working order and receiving the energy that they need, you will find that your body feels great, you can be true to yourself and to others, and you will show the right amount of love that you need. Your life is basically going to be balanced as well without any of the common ailments that most people complain about.

On the other hand, you need to spend some time working on your chakras if something isn't working out the way that you want. If you feel that you are dealing with bouts of anger and jealousy all the time, if you have pain around the body, or your focus is all out of order, it means that one or more of your chakras are not working the way that they should.

These chakras can also work together. If you find that one is not working properly, is not open the way that it should, and you don't fix it right away, you will eventually have the rest of the chakras go out of line as well. You need to focus on the chakra or two that are bothering you, and then the rest of them can start to align themselves properly as well.

Each of the chakras is going to have different levels of activity. When the chakras are open and allowing the energy to come through, the chakras are considered to be operating in their normal fashion.

Ideally, all of the chakras will contribute to our being. We all have instincts and if they are working properly, they will help to influence our thinking and our feelings. However, this is not usually the case because the chakras, and our intuition, will not be working properly. Some of the chakras may not be opened up like they should. When one or two chakras are down, all the other ones are going to become overactive and this can cause as many issues as well.

In the ideal state, all of the chakras will work together and be balanced. But with our modern lives, we are going to find it is harder to live a life where the chakras are in good working order. We are always on the run, trying to get things all done and barely being able to take care of ourselves. But if you want to really enjoy a good life that is happy and healthy, you need to take a step back, and learn how to take care of these chakras.

Luckily, once you realize which of the chakras is out of line and needs to be balanced, there are quite a few techniques that you will be able to use in order to balance out the chakras. Mostly, the techniques are going to help you to open up the chakras that are needed, because this will often fix up the issues with the other ones being overactive most of the time.

## The history of the chakras

While the chakras are part of an ancient tradition, they are starting to make a re-appearance again. There are many new interpretations of their meaning and their functions, and sometimes it is easy to get confused since there are so many ways to think about these chakras. While the popularity is starting to make the chakras more of a word that people recognize, there are a lot of times when this information is going to be erroneous, conflicting, and even confusing. Before you work on making the chakras a part of your life, it is important to understand some of the history that comes with these chakras and can better explain how they should be used.

The Vedas are some of the oldest written tradition from the area of India and it was recorded from the oral tradition of the upper caste Brahmins. The original meaning of this word of chakra is "wheel" which refers to the chariot wheels that were used by the rulers of that time. The word has also been used in these texts as a metaphor for the sun, which is able to traverse the world just like a triumphant chariot and will denote the eternal wheel of time, which also represents balance and order, just like the idea of the wheel and what the chakras are going to focus on.

The birth of the chakras was said to herald in a brand new age, and they were often described as being preceded by a disk of light, such as the halo of Christ, but there was a spinning disk that was in front of them. It is also said that Vishnu, the god, descended to Earth, carrying the charka, a club, a conch shell, and a lotus flower.

In these texts, there are also some mentions of the chakras being like a psychic center of consciousness in several different versions of this text including the Yoga Sutras of Patanjali and the Yoga Upanishads. The implied goal of Yoga was to rise above nature and the world that you are living in, in order to find the realization of a pure consciousness, one that was free from any fluctuations that came in with the emotions and the mind. Yet the word of yoga stands for yoke or union, so the realization that happens in between consciousness and realizations must ultimately reintegrate with nature to get a higher synthesis.

So, since the idea of yoga and the chakras arose inside of the same tradition, the Tantric tradition, it is no wonder that they are often associated together. As we will discuss later on, you will be able to find that yoga is one of the ways that you will be able to bring the chakras into line because they were both developed in the same traditions and both can be used at the same time.

In the traditional ideas of chakras, there are seven of the basic ones and they are all going to exist inside of your body. Through modern physiology, it is easy to see that the seven chakras are going to correspond exactly to the main nerve ganglia inside of the body, which all come from the spinal column. While many people assume that these chakras have nothing to do with them any longer, the chakras were well placed, put into specific parts of the body where nerves are located and where different parts can influence how the rest of the body is going to react. It is interesting that the chakras were able to develop based on these thoughts, even before all of the nerves and pressure points would have been realized.

In addition to the main seven chakras that most people concentrate on, there are a few minor chakras that are mentioned inside of the ancient tasks. For example, there is the soma chakra which you will be able to find right above the third eye chakra and then there is the Ananda Kanda lotus, which is going to be near the heart chakra, plus some more options based on how deep into the ancient texts that you choose to go.

Many people assume that the chakras are an ancient idea that you shouldn't pay any attention to. They figure that the chakras have nothing to do with how they live their modern life and they may assume it was all a bunch of spirituality that is just made up. But in reality, you will find that in modern times, the chakras are more important compared to any other time. We need to understand how easy we can get out of balance. We are always running around, always stressed out and worried, and often we have trouble with some of our own relationships. Chakras are able to get these back in line better than anything else.

People who practice balancing their chakras are often going to be so much healthier and happier, and better able to get through the day, compared to others who don't even believe in the chakras and just keep going through all of the bad things that are in their lives. It is definitely worth your time to ensure that you are able to get the great life that you would like without all the issues.

## The benefits of balancing your chakras

Despite believing that this is an ancient healing method that is not going to do a whole lot of good for you, the chakras need to be balanced if you would like to be in the best health possible. This is going to make it easier for you to feel good and to keep your emotions in check.

The benefits that come from balancing out your chakras are going to be closely tied with some of the philosophy that comes with yoga. If you have done some yoga in a class or on your own, you will be able to understand the full body integration that will come when you are done with one of these sessions. We are going to discuss some of the benefits of adding yoga to your routine to balance out the chakras later, but these two are closely related and will help you to get in the best healthy possible.

It is believed that when the energy of a chakra, or more than one of the chakras, is blocked, there are a lot of issues that can come up. It could lead you to feel pain and a lot of illness in whatever area is being blocked. It can make you feel unfocused, have trouble with relationships, lose your creativity, have pain, and so much more. When you start to practice the idea of the chakras and you work on fixing some of these issues with yoga and other methods, you will find that it is easier than ever to get everything to go back to normal and reduce some of the illness, pain, and other issues that you are suffering from.

## The types of chakras in the body

As earlier mentioned, there are about seven main chakras that you will see inside the body and all of them are going to be important to your overall health and wellbeing. Sometimes, a few more will be counted, but overall, the seven are the most important. The main chakras that we are going to be dealing with here include:

- The root chakra: this chakra is all about being there physically and learning to feel home in a variety of situations. If you have this chakra open, you are going to feel secure, stable, and grounded. You won't feel like you need to distrust the others around you and you can spend time right here in the present, rather than in daydreams. If you notice that you are feeling nervous and fearful often, you are probably dealing with a root chakra that is under-active. If it is overactive, you may feel a bit greedy and materialistic and you are probably obsessed with being secure so you won't like change.

- The sacral chakra: this one is all about the feelings and about your sexuality. When the sacral chakra is open, your feelings are going to come out freely and they will be easy to express without you becoming overly emotional about it. You will be open to this intimacy and you may feel lively and passionate and there are no issues with your sexuality. If you find that you are unemotional or stiff, this is because the sacral chakra is a bit underactive. On the other hand, if you feel emotional all of the time or you may feel that you are emotionally attached to others; your sacral chakra is overactive.

- Navel chakra: the great thing about the navel chakra is that it is all about being able to assert yourself inside of a group. When this chakra is open, you are going to feel like you are in control of your own life and you will have a good amount of self-esteem. When this chakra is under-active, you will be timid, will miss out on getting the things that you would like, you will be indecisive, and passive. But if the navel chakra is over-active, you will probably be aggressive and domineering.

- Heart chakra: the heart chakra is about affection, kindness, and love. When you have this chakra open, you are more friendly and compassionate and you will be able to make sure your relationships are as harmonious as possible. When you have a heart chakra that is under active, you will exhibit signs of being distant and cold. But when the chakra is overactive, you will go to the opposite direction. You will probably be almost suffocating people with your love and often the love is going to have some selfish reasons.

- Throat chakra: this chakra is the one for talking and self-expression. When it is open in the right amount, you will find that there are fewer problems with expression of yourself and you could even use this expression as an artist if that is how it works for you. When the throat chakra is not working the way that it should and it is under active, you may not speak too much and you are probably a shy and introverted person. Telling lies can sometimes block this chakra as well. If you have this chakra being overactive, you will often speak too much, usually taking over the conversation and it can keep people at a distance from you. This can also be the case when you are a bad listener as well.

- The third eye chakra: this is the chakra that is all about visualization and insight. When you have it open, you will probably spend a lot of time fantasizing about things and often have some good intuition. If the third eye chakra is not working properly, you will probably have a hard time thinking things out for yourself and you may find that you rely on authority figures to tell you what to do. You are also a person who will get confused easily. If the third eye chakra is overactive, you may end up living in the world of fantasy too much.

- The crown chakra: this chakra is the one that is all about the wisdom and learning how to be one with the world. When you have this chakra properly open, you will be quite aware of the world and unprejudiced against yourself and others. If the crown chakra is underactive, you may not be very aware of your spirituality. You will also be pretty rigid in your way of thinking. If this crown chakra is overactive, you will probably think things over too much. You can sometimes become addicted to your spirituality and may even be ignoring some of the bodily needs that you should be concentrating on.

As you can see, there are different types of chakras and they are all going to help out different parts of your body. When they are working well together, you are going to be in touch with your spirituality, feeling plenty of love to others around you, lots of creativity, able to think about all of the different things that you should do without overthinking things and just being at one with others, yourself, and the world that is around you.

But when one or more of the chakras go out of order

or get blocked up (or sometimes they open up too much), things are going to start going out of balance and your mind, your relationships, and even some physical things are not going to work the way that they should. This can make it difficult to feel good and you may worry about how to get better. While most of us don't associate these issues with our chakras, often concentrating on one or two of these chakras will make a difference in no time.

The chakras are a great way to take care of your body and to make sure that your body and mind will work properly well with yourself, the other people who are around you, and even with yourself. It can take some time to figure out the type of chakra that is causing the most problems and then giving it the cure that it needs to open up and return your health to you. We will discuss some of the options that you will need, including doing color therapy, working on meditation, and even adding in some more yoga to your routine to ensure that you will be able to get the chakras back aligned and can help you to feel better in no time.

# Chapter 2: The Chakras of the

Now that we understand a bit more about the chakras, it is time to take a look at what each of them is about. There are seven main chakras, and when they are all working properly and letting in the right amount of energy, you are going to feel amazing. You will be able to handle what is coming your way, feel full of energy, and not have any pains, bad thoughts, or other issues. But, when the chakras are closed off or opened up too much (both of these can cause issues), there is going to be some part of your life that is suffering. These chakra points are going to form up different aspects of your life including your psychic abilities, emotions, physical health and more and they include the following:

## Earth star chakra

The earth star chakras are important because it is responsible for connecting you with the energies that are elemental to the earth. It is going to help anchor you to earth so that you feel more grounded and can think about things in a logical manner. Though you will find that with the chakras, you need to acknowledge yourself as a Being of Light, there are times when you must be grounded in reality so that you don't end up with feelings and thoughts that are misguided. You also should find a way to be grounded so that you are able to participate in the here and now and so you can remember your highest path in life.

When the earth star chakra is not open well enough, you are going to find that it is hard to think about things logically. You may have your head up in the clouds all the time and talking to others about the decisions that you may need will seem kind of boring. This means that you need to bring in some more of that grounding to help yourself feel better and so that you can concentrate on your daily life. On the other hand, when the star chakra is opened up too much, you may be dealing with issues of thinking things through too much or feeling too grounded and worried about the things that are going on in your life.

This chakra is going to be found beneath your feet. The colors that come with this chakra include maroon, black, and silver. You can choose crystals and gemstones of these colors to help you with healing the earth stone chakra and garnet, tiger's eye, hematite, and onyx will all help with this one.

**The root chakra**

The next chakra is the root chakra. This is the source of your usable physical energy and it is responsible for anchoring this energy into your physical being. This is the region that will be in charge of relationships, especially how they relate to you inside a group, survival issues, and family. It is basically considered the foundation chakra because it is responsible for all the qualities and aspects of your physical well-being. The root chakra is going to be found right out the base of the spine, at the part that spirals right to the earth star chakra. The color of the root chakra is red and its element is earth. It even has its own note; the G right below the middle C.

When you see that your root chakra is strong, your abilities of smell and touch will be strong as well and your sense of smell can work as a psychic ability to you. This means that you may be able to feel and smell unseen entities, which others who don't have a strong root chakra will not understand.

If you would like to complement some of the energies that are coming out of the root chakra, it is a good idea to wear gemstones for healing and extra motivation including the red quartz, red jasper, garnet, tourmaline, bloodstone, or ruby. When the root chakra is working properly, it is responsible for healing the circulatory and skeletal systems, your hips, skin, feet, legs, kidneys and more and when it is used in the proper way, it helps you to understand how the world is connected because it allows you to be more grounded and even stronger when you are facing things you are uncertain about.

## Sacral chakra

The sacral chakra is the one that is located right in the lower stomach and it is the one that helps with your ability to connect with others and to experience adventures. It can also be associated with sexuality, abundance, well-being, and a sense of pleasure. This is a very emotional chakra because it is going to be responsible for how you are able to relate to others. It is associated with your sexual energy and your creativity, plus it helps you to look within yourself in order to understand and interpret what others are saying.

You will be able to find the sacral chakra by looking just a few inches below the navel and it is associated with the color of orange, so gemstones that are amber, carnelian, and coral will work great. If you are dealing with some issues in the large intestine, the bladder, kidneys, lymphatic system, reproductive organs, or the lower back, the sacral chakra is the one that you need to concentrate on.

## Solar plexus chakra

The solar plexus chakra is going to be located near the upper abdomen and it is the one that shows whether you are able to be confident and in control of your life while also dealing with any issues that can come off about your self-worth and your self-esteem. If this chakra is having some issues, you may fee low self-esteem, have a bad day, or feel bad about yourself in some other ways.

Those who are feeling a lot of low self-esteem may be dealing with a solar plexus that is not working that great. This is the chakra that is going to help you feel like there is a higher sense of self and it will strengthen the integrity and the honor that you feel, as well as how to empower others as well. This one is connected and related to your mental energy because it is going to give you the ability to make good decisions and often, it is connected with your intuition. It will ensure that you are able to handle some of these emotional energies as well.

If you are looking for the solar plexus, it is located right below the sternum and about two inches above the navel. The color that is connected to the solar plexus chakra is yellow and the element in nature will be fire. If you have a solar plexus chakra that is healthy and active, it means that your gut instincts often work and they are active and that you have a good sense of sight. The gemstones that work the best for the solar plexus chakra include amber, tiger's eyes, gold topaz, and many crystals that have a gold or yellow tint to them.

If you are dealing with an ailment in your digestive system, the activation of the solar plexus chakra is going to help you out, especially when it comes to your pancreas, gallbladder, stomach, small intestine, and liver. When this chakra is balanced, this chakra is going to help you feel brave, generous, self-disciplined, and gives you a lot of confidence with some good ethics. It basically makes you a warrior. But if it is not working well, you will feel that you are without a personal identity, you give too much to others when it isn't necessary, and you just can't get that self-esteem off the floor.

## Heart chakra

As you can guess from the name, the heart chakras have to do with how much you are able to love others around you. You will be able to find this chakra right in the middle of the chest, above the heart. Not only does it help you with love, it can help with healing, peace, and joy. This is the chakra that focuses on compassion, forgiveness, and love. Whatever pain that you are feeling that is emotional is going to transform you based on the circumstances. Because this chakra is right in the middle of the body, it focuses on love as its own basis of living. This chakra will be associated with green and pink and your sense of touch will become more sensitive when you have this chakra working properly.

In addition to helping you with love and caring for others, the heart chakra is great for helping all parts of the respiratory system. This would include the parts of the diaphragm, the heart, and the lungs. As the name suggests, the mantra for this one is that love is always the highest power. Above all, love is so important and it is a form of respect as well as of care that you can give to others and to yourself.

When the heart chakra is working properly, you will feel hope, compassion, dedication, peace, and even kindness to those around you. But when the heart chakra is not given the attention that it needs, it is easier to feel times of jealousy and anger. Resentment can often bubble up to the surface and it becomes hard to forgive others. You can alienate yourself away from others and even become a bit secretive in the process. This is why it is so important to give your heart chakra the attention that it needs so you can feel all the good feelings and none of the bad.

## Thymus chakra

This is the chakra that will help you to reach the realm of unconditional love. This one can help you become showered in healing, wisdom, and divine light. Everything in your life will become clearer to you when this chakra is working and you even become more open to what others have to say. You accept other people for who they are rather than trying to get them to change. This is a very important chakra because it is considered the gateway to the highest life path, and it is where all intent is born. For example, whenever you feel angry, it is going to be the thymus chakra that will try to prevent you from saying something you'll regret down the road.

You will be able to find the thymus chakra right between the heart chakra and the throat chakra. The wellspring of your energy, this one is going to be associated with purple, green, and aqua. You will also find that many people associate this one to the endocrine system, the immune system, and the thymus gland. For this one, the white fire will be the symbol.

There are a lot of psychic abilities that come with this particular chakra. When it is in good working order, you are able to have lucid dreaming, as well as the power to be completely open to how others are. It is easier for you to express your own emotions to people as well as to express your own love to those you care about. But when the thymus chakra is blocked, there is not much power inside of you and it is easier to become manipulated by others. You will reject the help of others and your own spirituality. You become closed off and may have some issues with expressing how you feel and you will either judge others quickly or feel that others are judging you.

**Throat chakra**

The next chakra that you have is the throat chakra. This is the one that helps you to express yourself and to communicate the messages that you want properly. You can use this chakra to be more creative and you will have enough willpower, as well as the choices to make some healthy decisions. You will try to live up to your own personal honor and will keep all of your promises to other people. The throat chakra is going to help connect the heart and the mind and it is located right in the throat so that it denotes your ability to communicate, and is often compared to telling the truth and being able to express yourself well.

If you find that the throat chakra is damaged, you are probably dealing with a lot of feelings that are all bottled up inside. Often, these feelings are going to be ignored, but they can affect how your whole day goes if you don't give them the attention that they need.

Sky blue is the color that is given to the throat chakra. This chakra is going to concentrate on opening you up to the truth in your soul and to the wisdom that you need to know. This is because you are able to communicate with the throat chakra so it is the one that allows you to express yourself. It is located right at the base of the throat and it is going to help you to exercise your own willpower as the sustenance that your soul needs.

## Third eye chakra

This chakra is the one that will allow you to focus on what is going on around you and help you to see the bigger picture. This one can be found right in between the eyes on your forehead and is often associated with intuition, wisdom, and how well you are able to think. This is going to be the center of your intuition, your intellect, and your visions. If you have the ability to talk to and see spirits, the third eye is the one that you can thank for this. Unlike most people, you are going to be more sensitive to motion, sounds, and some of the other things that are going on around you that others may not notice because you have honed your psychic abilities.

With this chakra, you are going to be able to find and evaluate your own insights. It is going to use the wisdom that you gained from life experience in order to help you to make decisions. If you are able to allow this third eye to work, you are trusting in a higher power and it becomes easier to align yourself with some powers that you may not be able to see.

You will be able to find the third eye chakra right in the middle of the forehead, between the brows. The color that forms this chakra is going to be either an indigo blue or a violet. If this chakra is working well, you are going to be gifted with inner knowledge and you have the benefit of really knowing yourself fully. You may also have some other gifts such as clairvoyance and telepathy. Because of the location of the third eye chakra, it is going to work well with many different systems including the whole of the nervous system, the brain, and the head as well as your sense organs, the pituitary gland, the skull, and even the eyes.

When this chakra is not working in the proper way, you may feel uninterested in some of the things that you normally do or you may feel bored. You can become overly critical of others and a bit judgmental.

You will overthink things that are going on in your life and you often will lack the creativity that is needed to get things done. Opening up the third eye chakra can help to solve these issues and give you the wisdom in all of your choices that you need.

## Crown Chakra

This one is going to be located right at the top of the head, and often, it is related to your connection with your own spirituality as well as your outer and inner beauty. The crown chakra is going to be the one that connects you with your spiritual consciousness as well as with the Higher Self. It connects you with higher dimensions so that you can become more enlightened. This is one of the most important chakras in the body because it is at the top of the body, the easiest for the other worlds to get in contact with.

Since this one is located near the top of your head, it is going to have the color of purple, white, or gold. When this particular chakra is activated, your spiritual awareness is going to be awakened and you will become more attuned with the whole universe. You will start to live right in the present, rather than focusing on all that emotional baggage that kept you in the past. You also know when it is time to let go.

As you can see, the chakras are all going to influence different parts of your body and they are all interconnected. When one chakra is blocked and not working in the proper way, it starts to affect your life and the different aspects that are associated with that chakra. But if you ignore it for long enough, this situation can get worse and it can start to affect some of the other chakras as well. This is why it is so important to learn about your chakras and how to take care of them in a healthy manner.

# Chapter 3: How Do I Know My Chakras Need Help?

Now that we know a bit more about the chakras, it is time to recognize better when they are starting to have some issues. Often we are not in touch with your chakras, which can cause a lot of issues in our health and mental wellbeing. But since most of us don't realize that it could be the chakras that need some help when we are dealing with these issues, we will often just ignore them and don't give them the attention that we need to.

Each of the chakras is important and are going to take care of a different part of the body, a different system, and even different emotions. It is important to know when one of the chakras is not behaving the way that it should and when something is going wrong, it is important to know which of the chakras you need to fix. Here we are going to take a look at each of the problems that the chakras can experience so that we can learn how to fix them and make them feel better!

## Problems with the root chakra

The root chakra is going to suffer whenever you feel that you are not able to take care of your basic needs or when you feel that it is too hard to get your necessities in order. Whenever this starts to happen, you may feel like the prostates are affected, and you can feel issues with your immune system, the male reproductive parts, the legs and the feet. Because of these issues, you can also have issues with degenerative arthritis, knee pain, sciatica, and eating disorders.

As you can imagine, it is hard when the root chakra is off kilter and because it is no fun to feel all this pain in your legs and lower body. If you would like to get it back in balance, it is important to start believing that you belong here and that you have such an important role to play. Once you are able to get all of this back on balance, you will again be connected, supported, and grounded to the world.

## Problems with the plexus chakra

Whenever you feel that your self-esteem is low and that you aren't able to believe in yourself, it is because the solar plexus chakra suffers. It is also going to suffer whenever you are worried about criticism, especially if you had a lot of criticism in the past or when you are feeling about your physical appearance. When the solar plexus chakra is out, it is possible to feel problems with your intestines as well as with the colon, liver dysfunctions, high blood pressure, and even digestive issues.

When you want to get the solar plexus chakra back and working well, you need to learn how to accept yourself, no matter what. You are not going to be perfect, in your actions or in your looks, but you should just accept that these are a part of yourself. There are some things that you are able to do and some that you will never be able to do, and being able to accept these will help you to become more assertive and confident.

## Problems with the sacral chakra

This chakra is going to be affected any time that you aren't able to express your own emotions well and when you find that it is hard to stay committed on what you want to get done. It is going to be affected when you fear things too much or whenever you are giving in to your addictions. It can also be affected whenever you are betraying yourself as well as the people around you. These issues are going to cause pelvic and back pain, issues with your reproductive organs, and urinary problems.

When you are ready to get this all back in balance, it is time to stay creative, stay committed, and learn that it is fine to take some risks. You also need to learn how to be sexual, outgoing, and passionate. When you are able to add these into your daily life, you will be able to honor yourself as well as others.

## Problems with the heart chakra

When you love people too much, or too little, it is because the heart chakra suffers. It is also going to suffer when you abandon others, when you get bitter or angry, or when you become jealous. This is what is going to lead to upper arm problems, shoulder problems, wrist pain, lymphatic system issues, asthma, and heart disease. Who would think that such a simple thing as how much you love others will influence how many health conditions you are going with.

There are some simple things that you are able to do in order to get your heart chakra all back in balance. To do this, you should always make sure that gratitude, compassion, and joy are the rules of your life. You need to learn how to let the forgiveness flow and then learn how to give trust to others. When you are able to do this, when you learn how to love yourself and others around you, you will be more successful.

## Problems with the third eye

This is one of the most complicated chakras to work with, and it is not going to be an easy one to work with or get open. When you let the emotions you are feeling start to take over your judgment or when you start to get really moody. It can also become affected any time that your daydreams get out of hand and your imagination takes over your reality. When you don't reflect on the state that your life currently is in and when you become volatile, it is because the third eye needs some help.

To take some of this blockage away, you need to look at the bigger picture of your life, rather than spending all this time overanalyzing what is going on. When you can look at this bigger picture, you will get some more clarity and it is easier to focus on the different things that you need to get your attention rather than on other things that are not that important. You can even use this method to recognize what your fears are and then stop them from taking over your life, and you learn how to gain wisdom from others. Overall, when you are clearing out some of the issues with the third eye, you will gain more wisdom and insight and it is easier to appreciate the life that you have, even more.

## Problems with the throat chakra

You will notice that the throat chakra is the one that will be blocked when you aren't able to write or speak your thoughts out very clearly or whenever you feel that others are dictating what you are supposed to do. This can often happen when you feel that you don't have choices in the matter and everyone else gets to decide these things for you. This is the chakra that you will have to deal with when your body has shoulder and neck pain, ear infections, ulcers, facial problems, issues with the thyroid, and sore throats.

If you would like to get this one back in balance, you need to learn how to make yourself heard above the crowd. This means that you must speak your mind and make sure that no one else is determining what you get to do in life. When you learn how to speak up about your own opinions, it is easier to be a good listener, communicative, expressive, firm, and honest.

## Problems with the crown chakra

And finally, we need to spend some time working on our crown chakra. When this one gets blocked, it is often because you are trying to find a greater power than the one you already have, and you will have problems figuring out how to use your skills and your knowledge for the best. Sometimes, it will also become affected when you let religious and political problems bother you too much, or when you overanalyze, carry prejudice, or are scared of being alone.

If you would like to prevent the crown chakra from becoming blocked, you need to have some clarity of your mind and learn how to live mindfully. When you are able to do this, it is easier to live inside the moment and to have the wisdom and inner guidance that is true and unshakable. Of course, this is going to take some time to master and get down, but practicing some meditation and mindfulness each day can really help with this.

Now that we have some ideas of what can block up each of the chakras, it is important to learn some of the steps that you are able to take in order to clear them up. There are many things in our daily lives that can affect the chakras and when they are not taken care of, it is harder to live a fulfilled and healthy life that you want. But when you recognize the issues, it is easier to get them all taken care of in no time.

# Chapter 4: Using Color Therapy to Help Clear the Chakras

One of the ways that you can work to balance your chakras is through a process that is known as color therapy. This is a really unique method because it will use some of the colors that we discussed a little bit above in order to help you to get your chakras back up and running properly. Each of the chakras is going to align with a specific color or colors and you will be able to use these in order to help you to get the results that you would like. Here we are going to take the time to talk about color therapy and how you can use this to finally get those chakras in line in an easy manner.

**Understanding color therapy**

When we are talking about the chakras, we are talking about channels of energy that are going to run right down the middle of your body. There are seven main chakras that you will find in the body and they are going to keep each other in check as much as possible. Each of these chakras is going to represent a different type of energy and when one of them throw off the balance, it is going to have negative effects on both your mental and physical health, and the other chakras can suffer as well.

For example, if you are someone who suffers from the seasonal depression disorder, this could be blamed on a crown chakra, the one that is at the top of your head. Or if you are dealing with something like an imbalance that is inside of the heart chakra, it will manifest itself in many different ways such as a weak immune system or allergies.

In addition to the chakras helping to control how you feel and keeping things in balance, each of the chakras is going to be associated with a certain color. This is why color therapy has often been used to help restore some of the balance that has been lost with the chakra that was affected. Some people may be unsure about color therapy or they will assume that it just doesn't work, but you will find that using a pendant or bracelet of the color for the chakra, or choosing to just have a gemstone of the chosen chakra on the right spot for a bit will be enough to help you to get the relief that you need.

Here we are going to take some time to talk about the colors that are needed for each of the chakras that you want to work on. Each chakra is going to need a different option to help it out, so figure out the kind of chakra that is causing you the most issues and then use the right color in order to get the color therapy to work well for you.

# The colors that you need

## *The crown*

For this one, we will need to go with violet. The violet energy is able to connect to some of the feelings and thoughts that we are having, and it is really good to connect with the spiritual self of the person. When you are able to use the violet gemstone to help out with a blocked crown chakra, we are able to help bring out the creative side, help ourselves feel more self-confidence, and even to avoid depression.

## *The brow*

The color that you will need in order to take care of the brow chakra is the color of indigo. This one is going to help open up that third eye chakra in order to make you feel more faithful and highly intuitive to what is going on around you. Any time that you are dealing with troubles of intuition or space, you may want to use some indigo gemstones to help you out.

## *The throat*

The next one on the list is the throat chakra. This one is going to be in charge of your throat and your lungs and in addition to making things difficult in terms of the health of your lungs; it can make it more difficult for you to be trustworthy or to communicate to the others who are around you. The color that you will need for the throat chakra is the color blue.

## The heart

When it comes to the heart, you want to make sure that it is opened up enough that you are able to handle the love that you have with some other people and that it doesn't go too overboard when you are around others. If you need to fix the heart chakra so it isn't too over active or under active, you will want to rely on the green gemstones.

## Solar plexus

When it comes to the solar plexus, chakra is going to need the color yellow to help balance it out. This is because you will need it to lead to some more optimism, confidence, and practicality. Sometimes when the solar plexus chakra is not working the way that it should, it can lead you to feeling issues with the stomach and you need to add some more optimism and brightness to your life to get it better, and the color yellow can help with that.

## Sacral

You will find that the sacral chakra is going to be located right in the lower abdomen. And when this one is not working all that well, it is often going to be related to some issues of the testes, ovaries, and the uterus. When this one is open and working properly, you will notice that people are happy, independent, and sociable. Who wouldn't want to have more of that in their life? If you would like to work with the sacral chakra a bit more, you will need to check out the gemstones that are the color of orange.

## The base

And finally, we are going to talk about the base chakra. When we are talking about this one, we are talking about a chakra that is right near the base of your spine. This one is going to be associated with the bladder, kidney, hip, legs, and spine. These can cause a lot of issues with feeling grounded when it comes to it not working as well as you would like. The color that you would want to work with when it comes to this chakra is the color of red.

As you can see, the colors slowly change as you go down the body. You will have the purple and the blues up near the top of the head, in the areas where you would like to have a lot of calm and collectedness in your thinking as well as in your heart and your relationships. As you move down the body, you are going to work on colors that are hotter, ones that bring out more passion and happiness compared to above, because you want to have some passion in your stomach, your grounding, and even in your sexuality. Making sure that you have the right colors for the right chakras is going to make all the difference in how the chakras will work for you.

## Getting started with the color therapy

Now that we have taken a little look at what colors you

need to use in order to get started with actually being able to use the color therapy in our own lives. Some people choose to go to a professional, at least for the first few times, in order to handle the color therapy for them and to make them feel better overall. This is a great way to take care of your issues with the chakras and to ensure that it is all being done in the proper way. But it is possible to do the color therapy on your own if you feel comfortable with it or if you aren't able to find a professional who does this kind of therapy on their own. Some of the steps that you will need to take in order to get started with color therapy include:

- Find a place where you are able to be alone for at least fifteen to twenty minutes. You don't want to have a lot of distractions and other things when you are doing this.

- Now lie down on your back either in the bed or on the floor. You should have seven cloth swatches near you, ones that go with the seven colors that we talked about before that go with the seven major chakras that you are dealing with.

- When you are ready, close your eyes while still lying down and just relax. Take in some slow and deep breaths to get ready.

- As you start to relax a bit, take a look at all the events that happened for you that day, but make sure that you go through them in reverse order. Start with the moment you are in now, with you lying down, and then move back all the way to when you woke up that morning.

- As you are going through these events of the day, you will need to identify the major attitudes and emotions that you experienced or were exposed to in other people during the day. Think about what emotions were affected during these times, using a table if you need.

- When this evaluation is done, you should take the color swatches for all the chakras that you identified, and then place them on the part of the body that goes with that chakra.

- As you are lying there, with these colors on your body, visualize that each color that you chose is being drawn in through the chakra. Think about them all individually if you have more than one that you picked out. Let the awareness that you have a focus on the color being absorbed so that the chakra can start to heal a bit more.

- Make sure that through this process, you are taking in some deep breaths while you are drawing in the color from the swatch into the chakra and then restore some of the balance. You will need to spend a few minutes on each chakra to help it get balanced.

- When you are done with all of the colors, no matter how many there are, you will be able to take a few more deep breaths and then get up feeling renewed and energized.

## Full chakra therapy

With the option above, we talked about how we could help a few of the chakras when they may have had a hard time through the day. But if you have had a particularly rough time or you are just getting started with the idea of the chakras, it may be a good idea to focus on a full body color therapy so that you are able to strengthen all of the chakras that you have. The steps that you will need to take in order to do this full chakra therapy include:

- Take all of the color swatches that you had before and place them in the right places of the corresponding chakra.
- Breathe in deeply and let the body absorb the energy from all these different colors.
- As you are lying there and breathing in these colors, make sure that your focus is on the fact that all of your chakras are being harmonized, balanced, and strengthened with the help of the others. Feel, experience, and know that the entire energy system is starting to strengthen. Feel that the body is coming back into

balance again.

- You will want to leave these swatches on for at least five or ten minutes, or until you are ready to feel balanced, aligned, and charged up before moving on for the rest of the day.

## Other options with color therapy

Some people know that they have some issues with a particular chakra that they are trying to work with, and so they will use a slightly different method when it comes to color therapy. With this one, we are going to use a pendant or a gemstone and wear it such as in a necklace or bracelet, all of the time. This gemstone would need to be the color of the chakra that you want. You can then keep this around you as much as you need, wearing it on a daily basis in some cases so that you are able to get the full benefits of this chakra. When it comes to color therapy, you will find that it is one of the easiest methods that you can use in order to keep the chakras back in line and working the way that you would like. Whether you just need to work on a few of the chakras at a time or you are looking to do a full body therapy for all of your chakras, color therapy is often one of the best options that you can go with.

# Chapter 5: Does Yoga Work for the Chakras?

One of the most popular tools to use in order to help your chakras get back in line is to use yoga. Tantric yoga is one of the best, but any type of yoga can really help and will ensure that you are able to get the results that you would like from blocked or damaged chakras. This chapter is going to take some time talking about tantric yoga since this one most closely relates to the chakras, but if you want to learn just a little beginning yoga to get started, this can do wonders for the chakras as well.

According to tantric yogis, yoga is able to help you to get some improvement to your chakras because it is going to help you experience some specific differences in your life. Because of this, you are able to feel the new changes that come from within you. A good way to see this is the chakras as a spinning wheel because they will involve a convergence of the energies, feelings, and thoughts that come together with their particular physical bodies. Whenever this does happen, you will learn to separate your emotions from reality, fear from confidence, and your aversions from your desires. Yoga will be able to get all of this back in order, and if there are some issues with a chakra being blocked, it will be able to unravel this so that you can reach that higher potential.

## The best yoga poses for your chakras

Yoga is really easy to learn and you are going to fall in love with how great it is going to make your energy feel, even as a beginner. Spending just a few minutes on yoga each day is often enough to help you to get the energy back, and the balance that you need to feel amazingly in no time. Some of the best poses that you are able to work on for your chakras include:

- The Warrior I: this is a good pose to use when you need to have a better connection to the earth. It is going to give you a good foundation to the foot. The hips are going to get a good stretch for this pose, which can help to release some of the stale energy that is found in the root chakra.
- Bound Angle Pose: this is a good one to help open up the hips and will bring some attention to the pelvic region. Stretching this groin is going to help to release this tension and helps that chakra to work the way that it should.
- Navasana: this one is also called the Boat Pose and it is going to be used to stimulate your third chakra. This one is going to be located with your solar plexus and the

Navasana is going to activate the fire from Manipura while also helping us to connect with our own center.

- Camel pose: this one is great for opening up the heart center. It is common for many people to protect their hearts while also closing them off to vulnerability, but this is going to limit the experiences that we have on a daily basis. When we use the Camel Pose to help us with our heart chakra, we are exposing our hearts so that we can invite and give out more love.

- Fish Pose: this is a good one to release the throat chakra. When we take the time to stretch out the throat, it is going to make it easier to express ourselves freely through our own unique voices, rather than relying on others to make decisions all the time for us.

- Child's pose: this is a really simple pose, but it is going to connect the third eye right to the floor and will help to stimulate the intuition center in our bodies. By activating and bringing some awareness to this chakra, we are going to have a better access to our own great inner wisdom. You can also stack the first under the third eye while doing this pose to help bring out some more stimulation.

- Headstand: this one is a bit harder to do for a lot of people, but when you do, it is going to activate the crown chakra because it places some pressure on the top of your head. This is your gateway to universal consciousness and when we stimulate it, we are bringing attention to this area, making it easier to connect to the higher self that we should be.

To get the most out of these moves, it is a good idea to do a sequence of them and make that your workout. Holding each pose for about ten deep breaths before moving on can help you to hold them long enough to get the stretch that you need before moving on to the next move. It is also recommended that you would go through this list about two or three times, maybe more if the issues are really bad with some of your chakras. This is just a seven move sequence, so it doesn't take too much of your time and can really make you feel better in no time.

Of course, if you are short on time and just feel like one or two of the chakras are giving you some trouble, it is also possible to just pick out from these positions above and get the one that you think will work the best for you. A minute or so in each pose can do wonders for opening up that chakra and helping it to feel better than before. It is important to listen to your body and learn when it needs you to make some changes or to understand when one of the chakras is not working the way that you would like.

The chakras and yoga were developed along the same school of thought, and in the same tradition many years ago, which is why many times it is expected that you would work on yoga a bit if you would like to see your chakras clear up. Yoga is a pretty simple exercise and whether you make this part of your meditation and rest each day or use it after some tough workouts, it is still going to give you the benefits that you are looking for. Try out a few of these poses on occasion, at least, and you will love the big difference that it can make for your overall health.

# Chapter 6: Other Techniques for Taking Care of the Chakras

Aside from the few things that we have talked about in this guidebook, there are quite a few other techniques that you can consider when it comes to taking care of your chakras and getting them back into the health that you need. Some of the techniques may not work for you depending on how your chakras are reacting and what fits your preferences and your lifestyle, but they are all safe, and trying them out may reveal some surprise cures for you. Some of the remedies that you can try out to take care of your chakras include:

## Meditation

One of the first things that you should try out in order to take care of your chakras is meditation. This is actually one of the most popular techniques that you can use to help repair the chakras because it is simple and can fit into many of the different aspects of your life. To make this work, you first need to find a place that is comfortable and quiet so that you are able to fully concentrate the mind and keep it away from the troubles that may be bothering you. Get away with any distractions including noises, accessories, gadgets, and other things and even consider being near nature to get the full benefits.

You can pick a specific spot that will help you to get started with your meditation, or you can just pick out one that is quiet and will allow you to have a few moments of peace before you need to move on with the day. The important part here is to focus on nice, slow, and deep breaths so that you are able to relax while also learning how to release some of the tension inside of your body.

## Rapid eye technology

This is a good one to use if you are dealing with stress, and this is the main reason that your chakras are not lining up the way that you would like. It is able to eliminate some of this stress because it is able to mimic your REM sleep. It will help you to bury all of your anxiety and fears deep into the subconscious so that you can instead move the focus to what is going on here in the present.

## Visualization

This one is similar to what you would do with meditation, but it is sometimes easier than meditation for some people because they are able to focus on something rather than just on their deep breathing. This one can sometimes be called creative visualization, because you will be able to imagine where you want your life to be.

With this one, you will be able to achieve any dreams that you would like, simply by imagining how you would look, feel, and more in that time frame. For example, say that you want to be done with school and with a good job in the next five years. You would close your eyes and visualize where you would be in that time. What would your office look and smell like? How would you look and feel when you reach your goals? Often, this is going to help you to feel a bit better and can give you something to focus on, instead of all the troubles and other issues that come up in your life.

Another method that you can use with this one is to just sit alone in a room and visualize that a white light is all around you, basically enveloping you from foot to head, cleaning out all of that bad energy that you are receiving through your day. You can get this bad energy from objects, from people around you, and even from pollution so let this white light just clean everything out. Each minute that you do this, you will begin to feel lighter and so much better about your life.

## Crystal healing

Some people decide to take care of their chakras with the help of crystal healing. Do you remember some of the colors and the crystals that we talked about in an earlier chapter? The idea with crystal healing is to bring these into your home so that you are able to cure the chakra that is bothering you. You would first need to pick out the crystals and the gemstones that would work the best for the chakra that you need help with, then create a little special place in your home.

Once a day, or when you need it, you would just lie down and then place these crystals onto the chakra region that you are hoping to heal. You can also wear these crystals each day, such as with a pendant or with a bracelet, and you will start to notice that there are some changes in your mood and in your body.

## Emotional freedom technique

This is a good one to use if you want to work on acupuncture. You would work with a professional who is able to tap the acupuncture points that may be blocked up around your chakras. When this is done, all of the unwanted energy in these points will be released. It is a good one if you have a lot of pent up emotions and would like to get them cleared up as well.

## Reframing the beliefs that you hold

All of us have some beliefs that we hold onto really closely and we figure that they are always right for us.

But sometimes, it is these beliefs that are going to make it really hard for us to have open and clear chakras. Sometimes, the beliefs are actually wrong or it doesn't really matter what they are about, because they don't matter to the current situation. If you are worried about some of those chakras being all blocked up and not working properly, it may be time to get rid of some of your old principles and find some new ones that are going to be able to serve you a bit better.

## Drink water and walk around barefoot

This one may not seem like it is the best one for you to follow, but it is a basic way to start communing with the nature that is around you. Nature is great for resolving our fears because we are actually a part of nature, no matter what we may have led ourselves to believe. Have you ever had a bad confrontation with someone and then taken a quick drink to feel better? This is because we are reconnecting with nature and allowing it into our lives.

This is an example of how nature is able to help us when we bring it into our internal lives. But our external lives would need some more of nature as well. This is why there are so many people who will take the time to go on a walk or spend time outside when they are upset or when they just need to get away from all the issues that are bothering them through the day. There is just something that our bodies and minds love about nature compared to all the trappings of the modern world, because it helps us to feel collected and calm.

If you feel that some of your chakras are getting out of line and you need something that is quick and effective at getting them back on track and feeling better, nothing is going to work as well as being out in nature and connecting with it again. And if that means taking off your shoes and walking around barefoot for at least a portion of the day, it may be worth your time.

## Reflection and some self-examination

This is one that may seem a little bit new to you, but it is so important to taking care of your spirituality and your chakras. With this one, you need to consider yourself to be your own detective or priest. It is a good idea to ask yourself a lot of questions. These questions are not to make yourself feel small or like something is wrong with you, but they are there so that you can start to realize a very important manner.

These questions do have the point of helping you to see how your behaviors and activities influence you and to see whether you make changes in your behavior based on when you are alone or when you are with others. If you are making some of these changes and you are able to catch them, there can easily be a few different chakras that are out of line, and you need to work to help them out a little bit.

The reflection part is going to be all these questions. When you ask them, you truly become able to see what is going on in your lives and whether you need to make some changes or not. Be critical, but not rough, because you really do want to find the real answers, the ones that will help you to get those chakras in line and start to feel better.

There are just so many things that you are able to do in order to help clear up those chakras and get them back into good working order. Every person is going to find that a different technique is more effective for them, so don't feel discouraged if one just doesn't fit into your plan right away or it isn't working out the best for you. Just mess around with them a bit and work down the list and you are sure to find the perfect one for you!

# **Conclusion**

Thanks for making it through to the end of *Chakras: Chakras for Beginners—The Step-by-Step Guide to Awaken Your Chakras and Heal Yourself.* Let's hope it was informative and able to provide you with all of the tools you need to achieve your goals of self optimization and fulfillment.

The next step is to start recognizing your chakras and how to get them back in order. We spent some time talking about the basics of chakras as well as where each of the chakras is located and what they are responsible for. We also took some time to discuss how you can tell when a chakra is down and blocked up, including information on what issues would come up with the individual chakras.

Once we had a chance to understand a bit more about the chakras and what they are all about, we moved on to looking at some of the best methods that you could use in order to cure them. This guidebook spends time talking about how to use color therapy, yoga, meditation, reflection, visualization, and more to help you to get those chakras back in order.

When you are ready to line up the chakras properly and get them to work the way that they should for you, make sure to read through this guidebook and learn more about chakras as well as more about some of the techniques that you can use to get them back on track.

Finally, if you found this book useful in any way, a review on Amazon is always appreciated!

Printed in Great Britain
by Amazon